# NEARING HOME

*Life, Faith, and Finishing Well*

## Billy Graham

W Publishing Group

An Imprint of Thomas Nelson

Published in Nashville, Tennessee, by W Publishing Group. W Publishing is a registered trademark of Thomas Nelson.

Thomas Nelson titles may be purchased in bulk for educational, business, fund-raising, or sales promotional use. For information, please e-mail SpecialMarkets@ThomasNelson.com.

ISBN 978-0-8499-6482-4 (trade paper)

**Library of Congress Cataloging-in-Publication Data**

Graham, Billy, 1918–
  Nearing home : life, faith, and finishing well / Billy Graham.
    p. cm.
  Includes bibliographical references (p. 181).
  ISBN 978-0-8499-4832-9 (hardcover)
  1. Aging—Religious aspects—Christianity. 2. Older Christians—Religious life.
  3. Graham, Billy, 1918– I. Title.
  BV4580.G725 2011
  248.8'5—dc23                                                      2011031734

*Printed in the United States of America*

13 14 15 16 17  RRD  10

# CONTENTS

*Acknowledgments*      v

*Introduction*      vii

Chapter 1: Running Toward Home      1

Chapter 2: Don't Retire from Life      17

Chapter 3: The Impact of Hope      33

Chapter 4: Consider the Golden Years      51

Chapter 5: Fading Strength but Standing Strong      71

Chapter 6: Death's Destination      93

Chapter 7: Influencing the Impressionable      111

Chapter 8: A Foundation That Lasts      129

Chapter 9: Roots Strengthen in Time      143

Chapter 10: Then and Now      163

*Notes*      181

*About the Author*      182

# ACKNOWLEDGMENTS

I am deeply grateful to all those who have encouraged me to write this book, especially my son Franklin and my editors at Thomas Nelson, David Moberg and Matt Baugher. My longtime associate, Dr. John N. Akers, worked with me to develop the manuscript for publication; without his assistance it would not have been completed. I am thankful also for the contributions of Dr. David Bruce, Stephanie Wills, and Patricia Lynn of my staff, and of Donna Lee Toney.

# INTRODUCTION

I never thought I would live to be this old.

All my life I was taught how to die as a Christian, but no one ever taught me how I ought to live in the years before I die. I wish they had because I am an old man now, and believe me, it's not easy.

Whoever first said it was right: old age is not for sissies. Get any group of older people together, and I can almost guarantee what their favorite topic of conversation will be: their latest aches and pains.

I will soon celebrate my ninety-third birthday, and I know it won't be long before God calls me home to Heaven. More than ever I look forward to that day—not just because of the wonders I know Heaven holds in store for me and for every believer but because I know that finally all the burdens and sorrows that press down upon me at this stage of my life will be over. During the last year the physical ailments common to old age really have taken their toll on me. I also look forward to that day because I will be reunited with Ruth, my beloved wife and best friend for almost sixty-four years, who went home in 2007 to be with the Lord she loved and served so faithfully. Although I rejoice that her struggles with weakness and pain have all come to an end, I still feel as if a part of me has been ripped out, and I miss her far more than I ever could have imagined.

No, old age is not for sissies.

But that isn't the whole story, nor did God intend for it to be. While the Bible doesn't gloss over the problems we face as we grow older, neither does it paint old age as a time to be despised or a burden to be endured with gritted teeth (if we still have any). Nor does it picture us in our latter years as useless and ineffective, condemned to spend our last days in endless boredom or meaningless activity until God finally takes us home.

Instead the Bible says that God has a reason for keeping us here; if He didn't, He would take us to Heaven far sooner. But what is His purpose for these years, and how can we align our lives with it? How can we not only learn to cope with the fears and struggles and growing limitations we face but also actually grow stronger inwardly in the midst of these difficulties? How can we face the future with hope instead of despair? These are some of the questions I have been forced to deal with as I have grown older; perhaps the same is true of you as well.

This book, however, isn't written just for old people. It is written for people at every stage of life—even those who never have thought much about growing older. The reason is simple: the best way to meet the challenges of old age is to prepare for them now, *before* they arrive. I invite you to explore with me not only the realities of life as we grow older but also the hope and fulfillment—and even joy—that can be ours once we learn to look at these years from God's point of view and discover His strength to sustain us every day.

Someday our life's journey will be over. In a sense we *all* are nearing home. As we do so, I pray that you and I may not only learn what it means to grow older but, with God's help, also learn to grow older with grace and find the guidance needed to finish well.

—BILLY GRAHAM

# 1 RUNNING TOWARD HOME

Teach us to number our days,
that we may gain a heart of wisdom.

—PSALM 90:12

Remember that as a faithful child of God you await
promotion.

—VANCE HAVNER

Growing old has been the greatest surprise of my life. The young live for the here and now. Thinking ahead seems to be in the form of dreams that promise fairy-tale endings. Though I am nearing ninety-three, it doesn't seem so long ago that I was one of those dreamers, filled with great expectation, planning a life that would satisfy my every desire. Since there were few things in life that I loved more than baseball, as a young man I dedicated myself to the sport and hoped that my passion for the game would lead me straight to the major leagues. My goal was simple: stand at home plate, with bat in hand, immersed in an important game. I often pictured myself hitting a big-league grand slam into the stadium seats and hearing the crowd roar with thunder as I ran the bases—*nearing home.*

I never would have guessed what lay in store. After giving my heart to the Lord Jesus Christ—repenting of my sin and putting my entire life into His hands—I laid down my dreams, along with my bat, and fully embraced God's plan by faith, trusting that He would lead me all the way. He did, He is, and He will.

As I look back, I see how God's hand guided me. I sense His Spirit with me today, and most comforting is the knowledge that He will not forsake me during this last stretch as I am nearing home. If that doesn't give me a sense of hope, nothing else will.

## MAJOR LEAGUER FOR GOD

I have remained a baseball fan, not necessarily of one team over another but of the game itself—the teamwork, the strategy, and the challenge of defeating the opponent. But baseball was not God's plan for me. Nevertheless, He taught me how to integrate these important components into service for Him. The Lord has blessed me with a loyal team of men and women whose hearts are united with mine—set on leading others to an eternal home with Christ. Our team strategy has been to fulfill the Lord's command to go into the whole world and preach Christ for the purpose of defeating the opponent—Satan.

When I started preaching, it was never my intention to preach inside a baseball stadium or any other stadium for that matter. I was accustomed to preaching in churches when I was pastoring and in auditoriums when I was traveling with Youth for Christ (YFC). At the close of the war in 1945, several of us on the YFC team had the privilege of preaching at Soldier Field in Chicago.

The details are sketchy now, but I recall the first time I stood in an outdoor arena to preach the Gospel. I had been invited to hold an evangelistic citywide meeting in Shreveport, Louisiana. When the local auditorium could not hold the crowds, the organizers had no choice but to move the event outside. Uncertain as to how people would feel about attending an evangelistic rally in a large arena, I was rather nervous. Then I thought about my boyhood dreams. Instead of bat in hand at home plate, I had what I now know is a much greater privilege: to stand behind a pulpit, with Bible in hand, immersed in the power of the Holy Spirit. I was not performing before fan-filled bleachers but pronouncing the Word of God to sin-filled hearts searching for truth.

Life, indeed, is full of surprises.

Now, all these years later, I still enjoy watching a batter successfully cross home plate, but nothing thrills me more than seeing the Holy Spirit at work in hearts as the Gospel is carried into stadiums, across the airwaves, and around the world. A baseball may be driven into the farthest corner of the largest stadium, but the Word of God travels to the farthest corners of the earth, proclaiming the Good News of salvation. It still excites me just to think about the impact.

Jesus Christ did conquer death, and by His resurrection He

was victorious. Before He left earth, He imparted to His follow-ers the greatest of all strategies: go into the world and preach the Gospel. After listening to His words, they looked up to see their Savior *nearing home.*

I wonder. What home are you preparing for? Some people spend their lives building ultimate dream homes so they can enjoy their twilight years. Some find themselves exchanging their bank accounts for residence within the gates of a retirement center. Others spend their last days in nursing homes. For those of you who do not know Him, choosing your eternal home is the most important decision you will ever make. For the Christian the last mile of the way is a testimony to God's faithfulness, for He said, "I go to prepare a place for you" (John 14:2 NKJV).

Regardless of where you lay your head at night, I hope your thoughts are about nearing home, and I'd like to explore those thoughts with you in the pages ahead.

Someone once said, "The gift of old age is remembrance." Although I have had to curtail most of my travel, life itself still keeps me motivated as I watch God's hand at work, not only in my own life but also in the lives of those around me and throughout the world. These last few years have brought the gift of obser-vation and reflection. While that may sound dreadful to some, reflection is biblical:

Remember all the way which the LORD your God has led. (Deuteronomy 8:2 NASB)

Remember . . . hold it fast. (Revelation 3:3)

Remember and do all My commandments. (Numbers 15:40 NKJV)

Remember the word . . . of the LORD. (Joshua 1:13 NKJV)

Remember His marvelous works which He has done. (1 Chronicles 16:12 NKJV)

These are remembrances worth recalling time and again.

I often hear people younger than me talk about their sleepless nights. There are times I experience the same. But then I remember those marvelous works He has done, and I recall what the psalmist poetically penned:

> When I remember You on my bed,
> I meditate on You in the night watches.
> Because You have been my help,
> Therefore in the shadow of Your wings I will rejoice.
> My soul follows close behind You;
> Your right hand upholds me. (Psalm 63:6–8 NKJV)

There is great comfort available, even to the aged, when we remember Him.

Not only does the Lord instruct us to remember, but the Bible reveals what the Lord Himself remembers—and what He chooses not to remember. "He remembers that we are dust" (Psalm 103:14 NKJV); and to those who are repentant He says, "Their sin I will remember no more" (Jeremiah 31:34 NKJV). I am so glad I can remember that promise. Because I have repented of my sin, God chooses to forget my sin. This is a glimpse into the heart of our Savior.

The Old Testament is filled with such remembrances. It even says, "Remember the former things of old" (Isaiah 46:9 NKJV). Society today may not like the word *old*, yet young people pay a small fortune for jeans that look old. Collectors put the highest value on antiques because they are . . . old! Others buy old clunkers, restore them, and then proudly drive down the highway showing off . . . the old.

The days when the aged were admired, looked up to, and respected are gone. Growing up, I was taught to look up to my elders, but there were only a few whom I considered to be ancient. I didn't really know my grandparents (except for a grandmother who died while I was in elementary school), so I had little opportunity to observe any close relatives who were well along in years. Perhaps the oldest person in our family I can remember seeing regularly was an uncle who often came to our house for Sunday dinner. As I recall, he was a janitor at the county courthouse in Charlotte, and I always looked forward to his visits because he usually had some interesting stories to tell about local politics and other happenings around the courthouse. To me he seemed old (although he couldn't have been much more than sixty since he was still working), so if someone had asked me then if I thought I would ever be as old as my uncle, I probably would have said, "No way."

As far as I know, few members of my extended family lived much beyond seventy; my father passed away at the age of seventy-four after suffering a series of debilitating strokes. Following our

1957 crusade in New York City—a demanding sixteen-week marathon of meetings that left me physically drained—I told some of my associates that because of the intense, nonstop pace of our work I didn't expect to live beyond fifty (I was thirty-eight at the time). Repeated physical problems in the years that followed—some minor, but others more serious—also made me doubt if I would live a normal life span. The added problems of middle age only seemed to support my theory.

And yet God in His goodness had other plans for me.

I am not sure exactly when it happened, but as the years passed, it gradually dawned on me that I was growing older. Middle age—I had to admit—was fading into the distance, and I was rapidly approaching what we politely call the *mature* years. Sometimes my age showed itself in small (even humorous) ways: the occasional embarrassment of forgetting a good friend's name, the reluctant awareness that most of the people I saw on an airplane or passed in the street were looking extremely young, the experience of having a server in a restaurant give me the senior discount before asking if I qualified. But it also revealed itself in larger, more serious ways: a slow but inexorable decline in energy, illnesses that easily could have ended in disability or even death, the obvious aging—and even death—of people I had known most of my life, my wife Ruth's brave but difficult struggles as the years passed and she grew increasingly frail.

I began relating to stories I heard from others. "Most of my middle-aged patients are in denial," a doctor said to one of my associates. "They think they'll always be able to play strenuous sports or travel anywhere they want or continue working twelve hours a day. They just assume if something goes wrong, I'll be able to fix it. But one day they're going to wake up and discover they can't do everything they once did. Someday they'll be old, and they won't like it because they aren't emotionally prepared for it."

I can't truthfully say that I have liked growing older. At times I wish I could still do everything I once did—but I can't. I wish I didn't have to face the infirmities and uncertainties that seem to be part of this stage of life—but I do. "Don't get old!" I've said with tongue in cheek to more than one person in recent years. But of course that is not an option; old age is inevitable if we live long enough. And old age definitely has its downsides; it would be dishonest to say otherwise.

The Bible doesn't hide the negative side of getting older—nor should we. One of the most poetic (and yet candid) descriptions in all literature of the infirmities of old age comes from the pen of the writer of Ecclesiastes in the Old Testament. After surveying the futility of life without God, he urges his readers to commit their lives to Him while they are still young. The reason? Not only would God give meaning and joy to their lives right now, but if they delay too long, it will be too late to enjoy God's good gifts. Turn to God now, he urges,

> before the days of trouble come
>> and the years approach when you will say,
>> "I find no pleasure in them"—
> before the sun and the light
>> and the moon and the stars grow dark,
>> and the clouds return after the rain;

when the keepers of the house tremble,
 and the strong men stoop,
when the grinders cease because they are few,
 and those looking through the windows grow dim . . .
 the sound of grinding fades; . . .
[and] men are afraid of heights
 and of dangers in the streets. (Ecclesiastes 12:1–5)

Behind his poetic expressions lies the reality of age's toll on our minds and bodies: declining strength . . . failing vision . . . trembling hands . . . arthritic joints . . . forgetfulness . . . loss of hearing . . . loneliness . . . fear of increasing frailty . . . the list seems almost endless. "Nothing works very well anymore," a friend said to me with a sigh not long ago, and I can sympathize with him.

But is this all there is to growing older? Is old age only a cruel burden that grows heavier and heavier as the years go by, with nothing to look forward to but death? Or can it be something more?

## AGING GRACEFULLY

Even if you are familiar with the Bible, you may not recall a man in the Old Testament named Barzillai; our only glimpse of him comes from just a dozen verses (2 Samuel 17:27–29; 19:31–39). He was eighty years old, and no one would have blamed him if he had chosen to spend his remaining days letting others shoulder the responsibilities he had once carried. But he didn't.

Late in his reign King David was forced to flee for his life from Jerusalem because of a revolt led by his rebellious and arrogant son, Absalom. His desperate flight took him east, into the barren desert regions beyond the Jordan River. Exhausted and almost out of food, he and his loyal band of followers eventually reached an isolated village called Mahanaim. There Barzillai—at great sacrifice and life-threatening risk—provided food and shelter for King David and his men. Without Barzillai's assistance David and his men might well have perished.

After Absalom was killed and the revolt collapsed, David— out of gratitude for Barzillai's hospitality—invited him to return with the king and the army to Jerusalem, promising to take care of him the rest of his life. Think of it: an invitation to spend the remainder of his days in the comfort of the king's palace—and as a friend of the king!

But Barzillai refused. His reason? He said he was simply too old to make such a drastic change: "'No,' he replied, 'I am far too old to go with the king to Jerusalem. I am eighty years old today, and I can no longer enjoy anything. Food and wine are no longer tasty, and I cannot hear the singers as they sing'" (2 Samuel 19:34–35 NLT). Old, feeble, and deaf, even the invitation to join the king in Jerusalem—an opportunity he doubtless would have jumped at a decade or so sooner—held no attraction for him. Old age had taken its toll.

Why does the Bible record this brief incident from the life of one obscure old man? It isn't just to remind us of the ravages of old age or even the brevity of life. Instead the Bible recounts it to tell us a significant fact: Barzillai's greatest service to God and His people—the one deed from his entire life that was worthy of being recorded in the Bible—took place when he was an old man.

When King David and his fleeing band of men approached, Barzillai easily could have said to himself, "I'm too old to get involved in this. Let the younger men help if they want to—they have all the energy. And anyway, I'd be a fool to take what I've saved for my old age and spend it helping King David and his men. Absalom might attack us and plunder our village if we assist David. Why bother? Why take the risk? At my age I have enough to worry about."

Instead Barzillai took the lead in organizing help for the beleaguered king. The Bible says Barzillai and his friends "brought bedding and bowls and articles of pottery. They also brought wheat and barley, flour and roasted grain, beans and lentils, honey and curds, sheep, and cheese from cows' milk for David and his people to eat" (2 Samuel 17:28–29). Think of all the organization and sacrifice that must have gone into this effort! Barzillai saw a need, and he did everything he could to meet it in spite of his age and infirmities. If he had failed or if he had refused to help, David and his men might well have perished in the inhospitable desert beyond the Dead Sea—and the subsequent history of God's people would have been vastly different. But he didn't fail, and King David's life was spared.

The point is this: as an old man Barzillai couldn't do everything he once did—but he did what he could, and God used his efforts. The same can be true of us as we grow older.

## That Great Cloud of Witnesses

Barzillai is not the only person in the Bible who made his greatest contribution in his latter years. In fact, Scripture is filled with examples of men and women whom God used late in life, often with great impact.

In the centuries before Noah and the flood, the Bible tells us, God gave great longevity to His servants. Adam lived a total of 930 years; Methuselah—the oldest person in the Bible and the grandfather of Noah—died at the age of 969. All of his life Methuselah's father, Enoch, had been a remarkable example to his son of what it meant to have a close relationship with God; the Bible says, "Enoch lived 365 years, walking in close fellowship with God. Then one day he disappeared, because God took him" (Genesis 5:23–24 NLT).

Enoch's godly example influenced not only his son but also his descendants long after his lifetime. Few greater examples of faith can be found in the Bible than that of Enoch's great-grandson, Noah. In the midst of a generation that scorned God and gave themselves over to every sin imaginable, the Bible says that "Noah was a righteous man, blameless among the people of his time, and he walked with God" (Genesis 6:9). When God commanded him to begin building his ark, Noah was more than five hundred years old.

After the flood (through which God brought judgment on the rebellious world and provided the means by which life could start again), God chose another old man, Abram (or Abraham, as he would later be known), to carry on His purposes. Abram was called by God to be the founder of the nation through whom the Messiah would come, the Savior of the human race. He was seventy-five years old when God first called him, and it wasn't until he was one hundred that his son Isaac was born, "in his old age, at the very time God had promised him" (Genesis 21:2).

The Bible is dotted with other examples of individuals whom God used in their latter years—men and women who refused to use old age as an excuse to ignore what God wanted them to do. Moses was eighty when God called him to leave the Sinai desert and return to Egypt to lead the Jewish people out of slavery; he remained their leader until his death forty years later. Joshua, his successor, was around eighty when God gave him the responsibility of leading the people into the promised land, and Joshua continued serving until his death at 110. Although Jeremiah was a young man when God first called him to be a prophet, he stayed faithful to his calling until his death (probably in his nineties), in spite of opposition and war.

The New Testament likewise gives numerous examples of men and women who were used of God in their old age. When God announced to Zechariah that his wife, Elizabeth, would give birth to John the Baptist, the forerunner of the Messiah, he didn't believe it at first. The reason, he said, was that "I am an old man and my wife is well along in years" (Luke 1:18). But God used both of them anyway, in spite of his doubts. Anna, who joyously recognized the infant Jesus as the promised Messiah when Mary and Joseph brought Him into the Temple to be dedicated to God, was "very old . . . a widow until she was eighty-four" (Luke 2:36–37). The apostle John wrote the book of Revelation while imprisoned for his faith on the isolated island of Patmos; at the time he was probably in his nineties. Paul, writing from jail after many years of sacrificial missionary service, described himself as "an old man"— but also expressed the hope that he would be released so he could continue preaching Christ (Philemon vv. 9, 22). Numerous other examples could be given of people whom God used in their latter years, not only from the Bible but also from the pages of history.

## Joining the Witnesses

But perhaps you are saying to yourself, "Well, that may have been true for them, but it won't be for me. Someday I'll be old, and when it happens my usefulness will be over. And besides that, I want to take it easy when I retire." You may even be convinced those days have already arrived for you.

These men and women were not unique, however, nor were they necessarily the kinds of extraordinary, superhuman individuals who come along only once in a great while. For the most part they were ordinary men and women, and as such they have lessons to teach us. The first is this: old age may have its limitations and challenges, but in spite of them our latter years can be some of the most rewarding and fulfilling of our lives. It was for them, and it can be for us.

They were prepared—mentally, physically, emotionally, and most of all spiritually—for whatever old age would bring their way. That made all the difference. They were able to do what they did because long before old age came upon them, they were already prepared for its challenges. Old age didn't take them by surprise; they knew that if God gave them a long life, then He still would be with them, and He would have a reason for keeping them here. For them, growing older was not something to be denied or dreaded; it was to be embraced as part of God's plan for their lives. They were ordinary individuals—but men and women of extraordinary faith.

How did they prepare for the unexpected twists and turns of growing older? And how can we prepare for those latter years, no matter how young or old we are right now? To put it another way, how can we build our lives on a solid and unshakable foundation—one that will undergird us the rest of our days? God has given us the answers we need, if we will only discover them and apply them to our lives.

❧

## NEARING HOME WITH TRIUMPHANT EXPECTATIONS

While growing old has been the greatest surprise of my life, the greatest triumph is yet to come: experiencing victory over death that will usher me into the eternal presence of my Savior, the Lord Jesus Christ.

While society may not believe that growing old is a respectable phase of life, my prayer is that believers in Jesus Christ will walk the last mile of the way triumphantly, as Moses did when he died at age 120: "Then Moses climbed Mount Nebo. . . . There the LORD showed him the whole land. . . . And Moses the servant of the LORD died there. . . . Since then, no prophet has risen in Israel like Moses, whom the LORD knew face to face" (Deuteronomy 34:1, 5, 10).

This is a remarkable passage. While Moses was prevented from entering the land because of his earlier disobedience, God allowed him to behold the land of promise in his old age. I often wonder if God, in His sovereignty, allows the eyesight of the aged to cast a dim view of the here and now so that we may focus our spiritual eyes on the ever after.

God's Word records that Moses' successor, Joshua, "was filled with the spirit of wisdom because Moses had laid his hands on him . . . and [Joshua] did what the LORD had commanded Moses" (Deuteronomy 34:9). Even after his death, the impact of Moses' life lived on in Joshua, the great military commander for God's people.

What testimony are you passing on to others following you? Remembering what God has done for you will invigorate you in old age. Others are watching your actions and attitudes. Don't diminish the impact you can make; pass on foundational truths of God's Word so that younger generations will be as Joshua, "filled with the spirit of wisdom."

# 2 DON'T RETIRE FROM LIFE

Come with me by yourselves to a quiet place and get some rest.

—MARK 6:31

Don't resent growing old. Many are denied the privilege.

—UNKNOWN

Enjoy life—it has an expiration date" was the bumper sticker on an old red Ford Thunderbird convertible parked next to a shiny new black T-bird. The age difference between the two cars? Almost fifty years. I had to smile when I learned that in the backseat of that third-generation 1961 model sat a teenager and a toddler, the driver's grandchildren. The owner of the black car was his son—the three generations were on a family vacation. It brought me back to the years when my children were small and we would all crowd into one car. We understood what it was to "be close." For most families today, this is a thing of the past.

A friend of mine related the parking lot scene to me. As she talked with the grandparents, others congregated to admire the '61 Bullet Bird, as it was called back then. It also became known as the American Dream Car. John F. Kennedy was a big fan of these Bullet Birds and had fifty of them in his 1961 inaugural parade. I was fascinated to learn that the old car was the one getting all the attention while the new model with all the high-tech gadgets quietly took a backseat. Perhaps it was because no one was inside the newer model to show it off. But I rather think it was the contrast of seeing a silver-headed grandpa with two lively kids raring to hit the road with their grandparents. Then to learn that this car had been this man's possession for fifty years made it personally authentic.

For a world captivated by high speed and instant gratification, its fascination with relics, antiques, and well-worn jeans seems disconnected. Yet when Coca-Cola changed its one-hundred-year-old formula in 1985, there was a public backlash and demands for the original, so within two short months the company was forced to return the beverage to grocery shelves under the name Coca-Cola Classic, spiking sales for the soft drink company. The conclusion of the marketers was that the formula had stood the test of time. The trade-secret recipe had trumped the new recipe, as proven by the millions of fans who did not want the "real thing" tampered with.

What does all this have to do with getting old? Old is authentic.

Old is genuine. Old is valuable. Some say old is even beautiful. I was told about an elderly woman who said, "I wish I had enough time, money, and courage to get a face-lift . . . my face is drooping!" Her beloved husband said, "Dear, the most inexpensive and lasting face-lift is just to smile; it draws your features upward, and that draws people to you."

Well, not all elderly people can climb behind the wheel of a dream car or get face-lifts, but we do have the choice to be content with where we are in life. After all, the alternative is not to be here at all. Can we say with the apostle Paul, "I have learned in whatever state I am, to be content" (Philippians 4:11 NKJV)? I have to admit that I miss the days of driving a car, but I am grateful for those who take me where I need to go. My aches and pains remind me that I am not as young as I would like to be, but I am thankful that I am still here to talk about them and that someone is kind enough to listen patiently. The mirror doesn't lie, but I can smile into it because my dim eyesight camouflages my wrinkles. Even at ninety-two, my desire is to learn to be content. We should never get too old to learn or too old to smile!

A police officer pulled over a distinguished-looking woman, the story goes, and asked why she had exceeded the speed limit. The old gentleman sitting in the passenger seat laughed and said, "Well, young man, we were speeding to get to the place before we forget where we're going!" Getting where we are going is important. Equally important are those who are following us because they are on the same journey; they just don't realize it yet. The older generation may have a hard time keeping up with the younger, but let's remember that as long as we are still breathing, we are leading the way. The generations that follow are learning about growing old from us. Are we good examples? While we have all made mistakes and would like to turn back the clock to correct some things, we know this is not possible. But the lessons we have learned from our failures and successes can help those following behind. The impact we can potentially have on them can mean the difference between leaving good memories in our place or simply being out of sight, out of mind.

A teenage daughter of a friend of our ministry reflected on watching her grandfather die at home. She said with tears in her eyes, "I'll never forget the loving care Papa received from my grandmother. It taught me to care for the sick and dying. More than that, it taught me about living bravely in the midst of difficulties." There is much the young can learn from those who have traveled the distance. Likewise, the elderly would be wise to consider the contribution the young make even to our own lives. They will see our mistakes, and they will see our triumphs. We will hopefully recognize their struggles and accomplishments and encourage them as they face the unknown future. The Bible says, "To everything there is a season, a time for every purpose . . . a time to gain, and a time to lose" (Ecclesiastes 3:1, 6 NKJV). In times of loss there are lessons to be gained. Let's not miss the purposes of God even in times of sorrow and disappointment, for He is always with us on our journey.

I recall the story about a couple yearning to retire after many grueling years of work. Every year they had gone to the same isolated seaside town along the northwestern coast of the United

States for vacation. His career with a major airline had allowed them to travel extensively, but this was their refuge, the one place in the entire world where they felt they could truly relax. Nothing, they found, renewed them more than a brisk walk along the beach or a quiet dinner watching the sun set over the Pacific. When a cottage overlooking the ocean became available, they bought it immediately, convinced they had found their future retirement haven.

Finally the day arrived. The airline duly honored the man for his long years of service. The couple put their house up for sale and began the twelve-hundred-mile trek to their new home. They lived it up: long walks beside the crashing waves, the easygoing life of a small town, the freedom to set their own schedules and do whatever they wanted. Everything was exactly the way they had always envisioned it. This was living at its best!

By the fifth week, however, unease began to creep over them, and they knew they had made a mistake. Watching the waves crash against the rocks wasn't enough to fill the void left by their former lives twelve hundred miles away. After their few weeks of rest, frequenting all the restaurants, coffee shops, and stores began to lose its charm. "Is this all we're going to be doing for the next twenty or thirty years?" they asked. "What were we thinking to leave our children and grandchildren?" They were fortunate that the home they had lived in for thirty years had not yet sold, so they packed their belongings and returned home. The airline executive took on a part-time consulting job with his former company and commented, "I thought I was ready for retirement, but I just didn't think it through."

## TRANSITIONING TO RETIREMENT

Many people could tell similar stories. The old saying is still true: the grass is always greener on the other side. Retirement is quite different from a two-week vacation, and change is an inevitable part of life, no matter how young or old we are.

As the years pass we move from childhood to adolescence, then on to young adulthood and a career, probably followed by marriage and children and—eventually—the empty nest. Some of life's transitions are predictable although others may catch us by surprise.

Life is full of changes, but one of the greatest comes with retirement. Many look forward to it; others dread it. Sooner or later almost everyone who lives long enough will experience it. "I can't wait until I retire," a man in his early sixties wrote me not long ago—something I have heard hundreds of times over the years. Another told me, "My wife and I are still in our thirties, and our greatest ambition is to be able to retire when I hit fifty." In contrast someone said to me recently, "I'm dreading retirement. The company policy has mandatory retirement, and I'll have to step aside in a few years. I enjoy my work, and I can't imagine my life without it."

Reactions are different because people are different; however, for most people the end of the working years is truly a watershed event—a major milestone, marking not only the end of their careers but also the beginning of their latter years. Retirement is only one of the changes most of us will encounter as we grow older, but it is a huge one. Even if our spouses haven't worked outside the home, the transition may be just as jarring for them as it is for us.

We may picture the years following retirement as a time of rest and relaxation, and to some extent it is true. But they have another side to them: like every other stage of life, our latter years will be filled with repeated changes and transitions. The decision to retire . . . adjusting to a different daily routine . . . declining health as the years pass . . . the loss of a spouse . . . the need to move or downsize . . . increasing dependence on others—these and other events during our retirement years bring their own difficulties and adjustments.

And yet many people are ill-prepared for the realities of retirement, either viewing it unrealistically through rose-tinted glasses or refusing to think about it at all. "I never thought much about retiring or growing older," a retired businessman confessed to me once. "If I'd run my business with as little advance planning as I gave to my retirement years," he added, "I'd have gone bankrupt." "I thought I was prepared for my senior years," a woman wrote me. "As a single professional woman, I'd devoted a great deal of attention to being certain I'd be financially secure. But now I'm realizing I'm totally unprepared for the emotional and spiritual challenges I'm facing. Financial security isn't the whole story, I've discovered—not at all."

## RETIREMENT AND THE BIBLE

Work is a part of God's plan for our lives. Work is not something we do just to put food on the table; it is one of the major ways God has given us to bring glory to Him. The writer of Ecclesiastes declared, "A man can do nothing better than to eat and drink and find satisfaction in his work. This too, I see, is from the hand of God" (2:24). Paul said, "So whether you eat or drink or whatever you do, do it all for the glory of God" (1 Corinthians 10:31).

For most of His life, Jesus worked with His hands. "Isn't this the carpenter?" some of His enemies sneered, assuming (incorrectly) that an ordinary occupation such as carpentry surely disqualified Him from being the Messiah (Mark 6:3). The apostle Paul likewise worked with his hands, often earning his living as a tentmaker during his travels (Acts 18:3). In God's eyes every legitimate work has dignity and importance, which means we should do our work with pride and diligence and integrity.

But our work was never meant to become the center of our lives. That place belongs only to God, and when we allow our work to dominate and control us, then it has become an idol to us—and that is wrong. Someone who brags about working seventy or eighty hours (or more) a week probably thinks he is the master of his job—but in reality he has become its slave. In addition, because his life is so wrapped up in work, his identity or sense of self-worth—that is, his understanding of his value or significance as a person—often comes to depend on his ability to work. Unfortunately our materialistic society only reinforces this view. But God says you are greater than your work, and your work is only a part of His plan for you.

Does this mean it is wrong in God's eyes to stop working and retire?

It's true that the word *retirement*—especially as we use it today—isn't found in the Bible. For the most part people in the ancient world worked as long as they were physically able. They had to because there were no social security plans or retirement savings schemes to help them in their latter years. In addition, many people worked for themselves as farmers or fishermen or artisans, and they had to keep working as long as possible in order to survive (as is still true in many parts of the world). If they were unable to work, they usually depended on their families to care for them. Sometimes that wasn't possible, however, which is why the Bible commands us to have special concern for those who lack family support—widows, orphans, and people with disabilities. The psalmist wrote,

> Defend the cause of the weak and fatherless;
> > maintain the rights of the poor and oppressed.
> Rescue the weak and needy. (Psalm 82:3–4)

The only explicit reference to retirement in the Bible concerns the members of the tribe of Levi, who were given the responsibility of assisting the priests in the Tabernacle (or later, in the Temple), the center of Israel's worship of God. This included the maintenance of the building and the care of the sacred objects used in worship. Their responsibilities began at the age of twenty-five, but the Bible says, "At the age of fifty, they must retire from their regular service and work no longer" (Numbers 8:25). The reason isn't given, but presumably it was to minimize the danger (through physical weakness) of accidentally dropping something used in worship and thus damaging it or making it ceremonially unclean. It may also have been to give a new generation of Levites the opportunity to assume their responsibilities.

Today we live in a much different world, and the idea of retiring from our work and enjoying our latter years is very much a part of our thinking. Older people are often pressured into retirement in order to give employment opportunities to the young. There isn't anything wrong with retiring, and those years can be some of the best of our lives if we can see them as a gift from God. God rested on the seventh day after He had finished His work of creating the universe, and we shouldn't feel guilty if He gives us the opportunity to rest once our work is done.

## RETIREMENT FOR ME

The decision to step aside from my life's work of preaching was not an easy one for me. For years I had told people I would retire only when God decided to retire me—but what exactly did I mean by that? Slowly it dawned on me that I wasn't sure how I would know if God wanted me to step aside, short of a major health crisis. Somewhere I had heard of a well-known preacher who persisted in his work long after he should have retired until one day someone had to take him by the elbow and gently lead him out of the pulpit because he wasn't speaking coherently. I certainly didn't want that to happen to me.

But as the years went by, I began to realize that I no longer had the physical stamina to maintain the schedule I had once kept. After much prayer and consultation with people whose wisdom I respected, I began to shorten the length (and number) of our citywide crusades, moving from two weeks to ten days, then to a week, then eventually to three days. I also began limiting other engagements as much as possible to preserve my strength.

In time I turned over more day-to-day administrative responsibilities in our organization to my son Franklin, whose commitment to evangelism and extensive experience as president of a worldwide Christian relief and evangelism organization clearly qualified him to lead our work. In 2001 our board of directors unanimously elected him to take my place as president.

Still our crusade ministry continued, and although I found even a three-day crusade exhausting as the years passed, God continued to bless the preaching of His Word. How could I step aside in the face of this? Much as I feared holding on too long, I feared just as much stepping aside too soon.

My decision to retire from crusade ministry came gradually and, to be honest, somewhat reluctantly. But as I continued to pray and seek advice, I sensed God definitely was leading me to bring that part of my ministry to an end. No one is indispensable. I knew that God would raise up others (including Franklin) to carry on the proclamation of the Gospel. As a result, after much prayer I concluded that our 2005 Greater New York Crusade would be my final crusade, and as it came to a close, I had a definite sense of peace, knowing I had made the right decision.

This didn't mean I would never preach again; a year later I shared the pulpit with Franklin on the final night of his Baltimore festival. Even as I review this chapter, I am considering an opportunity to preach a brief message over the Internet (which some say could reach the largest audience in the history of our ministry). I also have more time now to do some things I have always wanted to do, such as meet with young evangelists and encourage them in their ministries. From time to time I am able to visit our Bible training center at the Cove in Asheville or the Billy Graham Library in Charlotte. I have also been able to continue other parts of my ministry, such as writing books and articles from time to time. But nothing thrills me more than hearing from others who are on the front lines. It is encouraging to see what God continues to do through others.

As the older generation we should be mindful of our responsibility to pray for others. Retirement should not put us on the shelf. We should use this time in our lives to rest from our labors but lift up others who are carrying heavy loads.

## RETIREMENT AND YOU

The question still remains: How will you decide when you will retire? Will you be like the couple who retired too soon? Or will you be like one man who built a large and successful business but refused to think about retiring or hiring a successor—consequently leaving his company in chaos when he died at age ninety-three? The most important advice I can give you is this: seek God's will concerning your retirement. It may be one of the most important decisions you will ever make, so why not pray and seek God's will about it, committing it into the hands of the One who knows what is best for you and your family?

"But how," you may ask, "can I discover God's will concerning retirement? What signposts should I look for?" I have no secret formula, but let me suggest three things God may use to guide you.

## Consider Your Situation

Perhaps your physical health is declining, or you find you don't have the stamina you once had. Even if you are in good health right now, someday it probably will change. Are there things you have always wanted to do before that time comes? Or maybe you sense you are not up to the future challenges you are likely to face in your job, challenges such as changes in technology. How is your financial health, including both your retirement savings and your health insurance? Has your attitude toward your work changed recently? For example, did you used to find your work interesting or fulfilling, but now it has become a burden? Your response to questions like these may indicate it is time to consider retirement.

## Consider Your Spouse

Don't make this decision by yourself; your retirement will affect your spouse just as much as it will affect you. If your spouse is still working, will he or she retire at the same time you do? If not, what will you do while your spouse continues working? If he or she isn't working, what changes will your retirement bring to your relationship? If your spouse is opposed to your decision to retire or doesn't understand why you are considering it, it may be best to delay your plans.

## Consider the Pitfalls

"Throughout my career I was surrounded by people I enjoyed working with," one man told a friend of mine, "and I always felt like I was an important part of the team. But now no one calls, and I feel like I'm useless. I dropped by the office a few times just to see how everyone was, but I almost felt like an intruder."

Loneliness, loss of purpose, depression, feelings of worthlessness, anxiety, fear of the future—these and a host of other emotions are common among retirees. Sadly, some find themselves unable to cope with their new situations, and a surprisingly large number of retirees succumb to illness only a year or so after they retire. "The death certificate I signed says he died from a stroke, which was medically correct," a doctor told me about one of his recently retired patients. "But I believe he really died of a broken heart. He just felt useless and didn't want to live any longer."

Be aware of these pitfalls as you consider retiring, and do all you can right now to prepare for the inevitable changes that retirement will bring. God doesn't want you to end up feeling useless and depressed; He also doesn't want you to make unwise decisions about your future. Don't enter retirement without careful forethought and planning or without the conviction that God is leading you, for the Bible says, "A prudent man gives thought to his steps" (Proverbs 14:15).

## RETIREMENT AND THANKFULNESS

Let's remember that many generations before us have been where we are today without the conveniences we enjoy. Those conveniences have given us more time to use on other activities throughout our days. Most of us no longer have to grow our food, carry water every morning, or travel many miles just to talk to a friend. Instead of being frustrated by technologies, let's be thankful for the time they give us to concentrate on His blessings. Considering all God has given can fill the hours—and it should. "Finally," Paul told the Philippians, "whatever things are true . . . noble . . . just . . . pure . . . lovely, whatever things are of good report . . . meditate on these things" (Philippians 4:8 NKJV).

❧

## NEARING HOME WITH THANKSGIVING

The apostle Paul wrote those marvelous words of hope to the church in Philippi while he was in prison. His living conditions were crude, yet he wrote a letter to his fellow believers in Christ to spur them on in the faith. Paul's captors no doubt felt they had *retired* Paul from his service to God, but Paul's zeal for his Savior spurred him on when he wrote, "One thing I do, forgetting those things which are behind and reaching forward to those things which are ahead" (Philippians 3:13 NKJV). Though Paul was nearing the end of his life, he didn't allow the past to hinder his future—he pressed on. In another letter Paul wrote from prison to his friend Philemon, he referred to himself as "Paul, the aged" (Philemon v. 9 NKJV). Yet he did not allow his imprisonment or his physical limitations to prevent him from encouraging and challenging others to persevere in doing what is right.

The Word of God should fill us with thankful hearts that God Himself has not forsaken the aged. Are you willing to be used by God regardless of being bound by physical ailments, financial constraints, or the loneliness of growing old? Out of Paul's need, he was reaching out to others. Think of Paul's restraints, and then consider the impact of his words: "For we have great joy and consolation . . . because the hearts of the saints have been refreshed by you" (Philemon v. 7 NKJV). You have the capacity to be a "sweet-smelling aroma . . . well pleasing to God" (Philippians 4:18 NKJV).

# 3 THE IMPACT OF HOPE

They shall still bear fruit in old age;
They shall be fresh and flourishing.

　—Psalm 92:14 NKJV

The measure of a life is not its duration but its
donation.

　—Corrie ten Boom

In old age . . . blossom at the end like a night-blooming cereus."[1] This statement was written by a missionary to India, the late Dr. E. Stanley Jones, native of Baltimore, Maryland. He made a profound impact on all those around him because of his extraordinary faith and service to others. Later in life his work was acknowledged by Franklin D. Roosevelt and Mahatma Gandhi. In spite of a stroke at age eighty-seven that disabled him and impaired his speech, he dictated his last book, *The Divine Yes*,[2] and addressed a world congress in Jerusalem from his wheelchair shortly before he died in his beloved India.

The night-blooming cereus (a family of flowering cacti) that he spoke of brings a beauty to the desert when it opens up at nightfall. Some say these plants produce fruit large enough for people to consume. Dr. Jones certainly knew something about blossoming in the nighttime of life and producing fruit in plenty; consider all those he touched along his way. His is a worthy testimony of living a meaningful life during the journey to eternal life. Do we, the older generation, do the same? Are we producing fruit that replenishes others, or do we complain about our circumstances and drain others who look forward to living full lives? By our attitudes, do we make the younger dread the inevitable— growing old? Many elderly people, without realizing it, taint the purpose God has for them: to impact the younger generations by exemplifying reliance on Him and hope in His unchanging promises. We should be content, for Jesus has said, "I will never leave you nor forsake you" (Hebrews 13:5 NKJV).

## WISDOM FOR THE OLD

As we grow older, it is easy to feel that there is nothing else to conquer, so some retreat to the golf cart or the rocking chair. Some say, "I've seen it all." Others brag, "We've been there and done that!" The truth is that we gain new experiences until we die. I can assure you that my wife, Ruth, experienced many things in her last days on earth. She experienced God's peace that He promised. There may be common experiences shared by those who grow old, but every individual has unique circumstances. Some are widowed; others have disinterested children. Some care for an invalid spouse; some grow old together. Someone said, "If I'd known I was going to live this long, I'd have taken better care of myself!" About the only thing that comes to us without effort is old age.

But old age does not exempt us from fulfilling our purposes in life. The psalmist entreated the Lord for blessing on a most noble task when he asked,

> When I am old and grayheaded,
>     O God, do not forsake me,
>     Until I declare Your strength to this generation.
>     (Psalm 71:18 NKJV)

We find multiple examples throughout Scripture, from the patriarchs and prophets of the Old Testament to the apostles and followers of Christ in the New Testament, of men and women who made a profound impact on generations that followed. And today, their words live on.

In the day that Israel was experiencing economic ruin, the prophet Joel declared,

> Hear this, you elders, and give ear . . .
> Has anything like this happened in your days,
> Or even in the days of your fathers?
> Tell your children about it,

> Let your children tell their children,
> And their children another generation. (Joel 1:2–3 NKJV)

The prophet is reminding the experienced, older generation to recall times past when they had gone through similar calamities and how, when they turned back to God, He faithfully restored them. Today as we witness a threatened economy taking its toll on our national lifestyle, how often do the elderly gather the young to teach them what they learned during similar times? Some say, "There's a huge gap between our generation and the next. The younger believe our problems have passed us by; that we have nothing more to offer."

We cannot make others heed what we say, but we can and should speak out for the truth and pray that the Lord will open ears, minds, and hearts to what wisdom has to say. The Bible declares,

> Remember the days of old,
> Consider the years of many generations.
> Ask your father, and he will show you;
> Your elders, and they will tell you. (Deuteronomy 32:7 NKJV)

Scripture says that the man who finds wisdom is happy, and "length of days is in her right hand" (Proverbs 3:13, 16 NKJV). This is not to say that the older generation has all the answers—we do not. Our responsibility as believers in Christ is to proclaim the wisdom of His Word. God has taught every generation, through blight or blessing, to look to Him as the source of all things. The greatest remedy to any challenge, including the generation gap, comes from the Word of God because when the Word of God is proclaimed, God Himself blesses it.

The Bible instructs the young to honor the presence of an old man and to revere God (Leviticus 19:32), but do the elderly demonstrate such reverence before the Lord? Are we examples for the young?

The apostle Paul wrote as an aged man, "I thank Christ Jesus our Lord who has enabled me, because He counted me faithful" (1 Timothy 1:12 NKJV). Then he advised Timothy, "Let no one despise your youth, but be an example to the believers in word, in conduct, in love, in spirit, in faith, in purity . . . that your progress may be evident to all. Take heed to yourself and to the doctrine. Continue in them, for in doing this you will save both yourself and those who hear you" (1 Timothy 4:12, 15–16 NKJV). Paul acknowledged that God had equipped him to speak these words of wisdom to this young man. Many today are declaring that Christianity should not be complicated by doctrine, and young people are embracing this belief while many from the older generations sit in silence. We should just as boldly as Paul advise those younger than us: "Hear, my children, the instruction of a father . . . for I give you good doctrine" (Proverbs 4:1–2 NKJV).

With careful instructions Paul also counseled his spiritual son to advise his elders in the faith, to grab hold of scriptural doctrines and teach them to the young *and old*. Here is a wonderful picture of God's truth impacting one generation to another. The aged can learn from the young too. This is God's wisdom; this is His master plan.

To all who read this book, my prayer is that you will sense God encouraging you to impact those around you, regardless of age. Look for the Lord's purpose in every circumstance and in every face or voice you encounter daily, for the time He has given you is not without purpose. Prepare for each day by asking the Lord to open your eyes to what is going on around you. You may feel lonely, but perhaps the Lord will use your smile to draw someone else close to you. You may experience pain, but the Lord may use your resolve to strengthen another who doesn't have the will to go on. We can reject the opportunity to be used of God, or we can seize opportunities to impact others as a testimony to Him.

## PAIN: A TOOL, NOT AN EXCUSE

While writing this book, I had the great privilege to visit with Louis Zamperini, a World War II veteran who spent two and a half years as a POW in a Japanese prison camp. At ninety-four years old, he traveled from his home in California to Charlotte, North Carolina, where he graciously appeared at the Billy Graham Library. For several hours he shook people's hands and autographed copies of the book *Unbroken*, his life's story.[3] The following day, he rode two hours to my home, where we had lunch together. It had been many years since we had visited. Louis patiently answered my questions as I asked him to relay his experiences that led up to his conversion.

When Louis was rescued in 1945 and was welcomed home as a war hero, he enjoyed short-lived celebrity, followed by hard times. Humanly speaking, he had reason to be bitter and cynical. His wife, though, persuaded him to attend our 1949 crusade in Los Angeles where we conducted evangelistic meetings and preached the Gospel for six straight weeks. When Louis returned the second night, instead of slipping out early as he had planned to do when the invitation was given, he said that the Holy Spirit gripped his heart, and he walked the aisle into a prayer room where he repented of his sin, giving his life wholly to the Lord Jesus Christ.

"Billy," he told me during our visit, "within a matter of moments my life was changed forever. Since that night I have never had another nightmare about my captivity. The Lord radically transformed me."

What happened in Louis's life following his conversion is a thrilling story. While I had to coax him to tell me all he has done since then, he gave glory to the Lord for using him, even now at ninety-four. Louis is one of those night-blooming cereuses. Still serving the Lord, he is investing the fruit of his experience in the lives of others, some who are his own age but more who are children hearing his amazing story as the historical accounts of his capture and rescue are being taught in public schools. Louis's testimony and the Word of God are impacting all generations with the spirit of hope, for as the Bible says, "Your word is my source of hope" (Psalm 119:114 NLT).

I wish everyone had the opportunity to sit and talk with someone like Louis Zamperini. He is an inspiration. It is true that not everyone has a story like Louis's to tell, and aren't we glad? When Louis was in captivity as a prisoner of war, he doubted that he would ever reach retirement age. He experienced the challenges of old age due to brutal treatment and lack of nourishment; his body began to break down. Most of us never experienced that at twenty-eight years of age.

For anyone experiencing aches and pains, think of Louis and others like him who endured unbearable suffering in their service to our country. Think of the apostles and other early Christians who were burned at stakes or beheaded because of their allegiance to Jesus Christ. As they did, find a way to use your uncomfortable situation to point others to Him. Then remember the Lord Jesus who came and took upon Himself our guilt and shame to free us from the captivity of sin. What a privilege we have to remind one another that we are blessed in so many ways and that we have the Lord Jesus to comfort us in whatever circumstances we must endure. Some of us may be bedridden or confined to a wheelchair, but we still have important work to do.

There is not enough room in this book to record the stories I have received from people who have graciously supported my ministry, some for sixty years. I have learned so much from them as I recall their commitments to pray for the work of the Lord. A young lady once mentioned that her disabled grandmother prayed for our crusade team until she died. She had written our names in her Bible. This is humbling. It is also convicting. What lessons there are to be learned from this faithful saint. God forbid that we should ever retire from prayer, the sweetest work of the soul.

## RETIREMENT: THE TWO PATHS

For those who are retired and still in good health, there are many opportunities for service. We should always be expecting the Lord to reveal His plans for us. Just because we are retired does not mean our work is done. Retirement provides us the opportunity to spend more time doing God's work, serving others in the name of the Lord.

So many people come to mind when I think of those who have retired for various reasons. One of those is my friend Mel Cheatham, one of the most respected neurosurgeons in the world. He had one of the busiest private practices in California while also holding a prestigious appointment as clinical professor of neurosurgery at UCLA. Highly respected by his peers, he developed new surgical procedures, wrote extensively for various medical journals, and was elected head of his specialty's state professional association. But then, at the peak of his career, he stepped away from his work and took early retirement.

"In the eyes of most of my colleagues, I'm completely retired," he told me several years after resigning his positions, "but in reality I've never been busier. What they don't understand is that I retired solely because I felt God was calling me to use my experience in a new way, which is what I've done. And these have been the most exciting years of my life." Now he travels all over the world advising hospitals and clinics in less-developed countries on how they can meet the medical needs of their people more effectively. He also writes regularly, using his postretirement experiences to urge doctors and other medical personnel to volunteer their services to those in need. Much of his work is carried on through Samaritan's Purse.

Far different is the story I heard some years ago about another man. An astute businessman with an impressive record of success, he was hired by a large but languishing company to become its president while in his early fifties. Within a few years he had turned the business around, not only reversing its fortunes but overseeing its expansion into a number of other countries. Stories of his success as an executive appeared regularly in business journals, and his advice on economic matters was eagerly sought by business groups and government agencies. In accordance with his company's rules, he retired at age sixty-eight, staying on for a brief time as an advisor to the company's new president but otherwise no longer involved in its affairs.

"I was totally unprepared for retirement," he confessed later. "I'd been too busy to bother with any hobbies other than the occasional round of golf, which was always business related anyway. The company had been my life, but after I drove away from the office for the last time, they didn't even call me. We moved, and for a year or so I kept myself occupied building our dream home, but once it was finished I didn't know what to do next. Now I play golf almost every day, not because I particularly love it but because I can't think of anything else to do. My wife says I'm depressed, but she doesn't understand how useless I feel. I hate being retired."

Admittedly you may not be a highly skilled neurosurgeon or a major corporate executive; very few of us are. But the contrast between these two individuals points to a very important lesson we all need to learn about our retirement years: the best time to prepare for them is before they happen. Beyond that, however, is an even more important lesson: No matter who we are, retirement presents us with two choices. Either we can use it to indulge ourselves, or we can use it to make an impact on the lives of others. In other words, the choice we face is between empty self-indulgence and meaningful activity.

Take the retired business executive I profiled previously. I strongly suspect that at least a dozen nonprofit social service agencies in his community could have used his business expertise to help themselves become more effective. They would have loved to have him volunteer to assist them—but he never did.

## DETERMINING THE GOAL

Does this mean it is wrong to relax and enjoy life during our retirement years? No, not at all; to say this would be to say that God doesn't want us to ever enjoy the good things He gives us—which isn't true. The writer of Ecclesiastes said, "However many years a man may live, let him enjoy them all" (11:8). The apostle Paul repeated the Old Testament's command for children to honor their parents, so that "you may enjoy long life on the earth" (Ephesians 6:3). God knows that we need rest and exercise and relaxation; after a grueling period of ministry, Jesus urged His disciples to "come with me by yourselves to a quiet place and get some rest" (Mark 6:31).

But if this is all we do—if our only goals during our retirement years are to enjoy life and have as good a time as possible—then we may well have fallen into the trap of empty, meaningless activity. More than that, we have forgotten one of the Bible's central truths: every day—without exception—is a gift from God, entrusted to us to use for His glory. This is true for your working years, and it is equally true for your retirement.

## FINDING THE KEY

What, then, is the key to a successful retirement? See your retirement as a gift from God. Retirement isn't something that just happens if you live long enough, and it isn't even a reward for your years of hard work; it is a gift from God. Once you understand this, you will approach your retirement differently.

God gave these years to us—however few or many they turn out to be—so we could do His will. Paul's admonition applies to every believer: "And he [Christ] died for all, that those who live should no longer live for themselves but for him who died for them and was raised again" (2 Corinthians 5:15). But in another sense God's will is specific and individual. His plan for your retirement isn't the same as it is for someone else's. Remember: He knows all about you. He knows what you can and can't do; He knows your gifts and abilities, which, after all, come from Him; He also knows what opportunities you have to serve Him. In addition, He knows your needs and limitations at this stage of your life, and He wants to help you cope with them.

Therefore, the questions we each must face are these: Will we seek God's plan for our retirement years? Or will we drift aimlessly along, assuming our usefulness is over and spending the rest of our days trying to squeeze as much enjoyment as we can out of life? Admittedly His plan for us may change as the years pass and our circumstances change, but no matter how far along we are on life's road, our constant goal should be seeking God's direction for what lies ahead. Remember: His way is always, always best.

Perhaps you are considering retirement; perhaps you have been retired for some years. Whatever your situation, seek God's will for your future. Pray about it, seek wisdom from others, search God's Word for direction, and trust Him to guide you. His will for you during retirement may not differ greatly from what you have envisioned—or it may take you in new and unexpected directions. But whatever the outcome, make God's will your priority for your retirement years. Then you'll be able to look back over your life and say with King David, "My share in life has been pleasant; my part has been beautiful" (Psalm 16:6 NCV).

## ENDURING THE UNEXPECTED

Have you ever heard the saying that when one door closes, another opens? There is much truth in this. The Billy Graham Evangelistic Association has a chaplaincy program called the Rapid Response Team (RRT). While we have always worked with Christian chaplains around the world, a great need arose in the wake of 9/11. My son Franklin had flown to New York to see how Samaritan's Purse could provide assistance. The greatest need he identified was for chaplains. People devastated by the cataclysmic attack were roaming the streets that had once surrounded the Twin Towers. Some sobbed; some stared up into the sky in a stupor; others walked aimlessly along holding signs with names and pictures of loved ones and friends still missing. They all had something in common: they looked lost.

Ground Zero was not an easy place to access, but Franklin began calling pastors and Bible students, asking them to come and provide spiritual help. We were overwhelmed by the response from people who had the skills and hearts for such work. Franklin had the vision to assemble and train battalions of chaplains who would be willing to go, at a moment's notice, to areas of the nation or the world where disaster struck. Today, many of these volunteers are retirees—men and women who want to reach out to those in need, open the Bible, and share with them that there is still hope through Jesus Christ, even in times of despair. Souls have been saved, and others, already believers, have been encouraged through spending time in prayer with these chaplains, receiving comfort that comes from above.

One man who had been a construction worker all of his life said, "I thought my life was over when I was forced to retire because of back trouble. I never dreamed that God would allow me to help people with greater problems than mine by going and praying with them and for them. When I walk through rubble left behind by a killer tornado, I remember years spent clearing debris from a construction site. Now I am able to help someone clear their mind by offering them insight from God's Word. My life has never been so fulfilled."

Volunteer service has become very popular in recent decades. Some companies even require employees to give so many hours a year to a volunteer agency. Better than that is when people do it because they truly have a desire to help others, not just fulfill a requirement.

Samaritan's Purse has taken a tremendous lead in this area, offering opportunities to many from various walks of life. There are touching stories about physicians who leave their lucrative practices to help a missionary doctor for a few weeks in third world countries. Multiple thousands every year volunteer to send out shoe box gifts for children through Operation Christmas Child. One retired couple decided to spend November and December in North Carolina to work in the warehouse getting the boxes ready to ship overseas. They drove from the Midwest and stayed every night in their camper so they could be ready for work the next day. They said, "As long as God enables us, we want to use our days like this. We are receiving blessing beyond measure."

Other retirees take advantage of learning more about the Bible in their years of retirement. An older lady attended a Bible study at the Cove and said, "I never felt equipped to talk to others about the Lord, but having the opportunity to meet others who feel the same way and being encouraged in the Scriptures have given me the courage to teach others. If I hadn't retired, I would have never explored this opportunity."

I would encourage you to pray and ask the Lord to show you what you can do as you transition your time and talents. Get involved in your local church and other ministries that point people to Christ. This will stretch you and challenge you to grow deeper in your own faith. Take to heart what Peter wrote near the end of his life: "But grow in the grace and knowledge of our Lord and Savior Jesus Christ" (2 Peter 3:18). In doing so, you help others do the same.

Whatever you do, keep your mind and your body occupied; don't give laziness or boredom a chance to take root in your soul. The devil delights in someone who is idle or bored; he knows this leads to temptation or discouragement. But the person who is occupied with worthwhile activities is far less vulnerable. Remember the Bible's admonition: "Do not give the devil a foothold" (Ephesians 4:27).

## WORKING WITH FEWER CHOICES

Perhaps, however, you are saying to yourself, "What you suggest may be fine for other people, but I don't have any options. It's all I can do to keep up with the problems I'm facing, and it's not getting any better." We never know what the future holds for us, but God does. This is why Jesus urged us not to be paralyzed by fear of the future but to trust our lives into God's hands: "Who of you by worrying can add a single hour to his life? . . . But seek first his kingdom and his righteousness, and all these things will be given to you as well" (Matthew 6:27, 33).

I often think of my father-in-law, Dr. L. Nelson Bell. For twenty-five years he and his wife, Virginia, served the people of China as medical missionaries. (My wife, Ruth, was born and grew up there.) He was one of the busiest people I ever knew—and also one of the most dedicated. One of my strongest memories of Dr. Bell was the way in which he cared for his wife after she suffered a series of debilitating strokes. She was confined to a wheelchair and required almost constant care. It would have been logical for Dr. Bell to move her out of their house and into a nursing home, but he refused. Instead he gave up almost all of his outside responsibilities and devoted himself to caring for his beloved Virginia. When someone asked him about his decision, he simply replied, "This is my calling now."

One day you may not be able to do everything you once did

or everything you would like to do. Instead of feeling guilty or frustrated or resentful, however, thank God that you can still do some things—and make it your goal to do them faithfully and do them well. Commit your time—and your whole self—to Jesus Christ, and seek to do His will no matter what comes your way.

## NEARING HOME WITH HOPE

This principle is what Jesus was explaining to Peter shortly before He ascended to Heaven. The dialogue between Peter and his Lord is one of the most direct yet tender exchanges in the Gospels. Jesus asked Peter, "Do you truly love me?" Peter answered, "Yes, Lord, you know that I love you." Jesus said to him, "Take care of my sheep. . . . I tell you the truth, when you were younger you dressed yourself and went where you wanted; but when you are old you will stretch out your hands, and someone else will dress you and lead you where you do not want to go" (John 21:16–18).

Jesus was predicting Peter's death, which would occur some forty years later. Peter recalled the conversation when he wrote, "I think it is right to refresh your memory as long as I live in the tent of this body, because I know that I will soon put it aside, as our Lord Jesus Christ has made clear to me. And I will make every effort to see that after my departure you will always be able to remember these things" (2 Peter 1:13–15).

In the face of brutal death, this old and faithful follower of Jesus was doing what Christ commanded: care for others. While Peter was preparing to depart his earthly life, he did not back down in reminding others what they should remember long after he was gone. What were these things? Peter had just finished telling them: "Add to your faith goodness; and to goodness, knowledge; and to knowledge, self-control; and to self-control, perseverance; and to perseverance, godliness; and to godliness, brotherly kindness; and to brotherly kindness, love. For if you possess these qualities in increasing measure, they will keep you from being ineffective and unproductive in your knowledge of our Lord Jesus Christ" (2 Peter 1:5–8).

Peter did not wallow in self-pity but immersed himself in the *knowledge of our Lord Jesus Christ*, a phrase repeated multiple times in the eight short chapters of 1 and 2 Peter.

You may still be an active senior adult, or you may be riddled with aches and confined to bed, but you can still be a productive servant of Jesus Christ by filling your mind with the knowledge of Jesus Christ and, as Peter did, impacting those around you with hope: "In keeping with his [Christ's] promise we are looking forward to a new heaven. . . . So then, dear friends, . . . grow in the grace and knowledge of our Lord and Savior Jesus Christ" (2 Peter 3:13, 14, 18).

# 4 CONSIDER THE GOLDEN YEARS

Behold now, I am old, I do not know the day of my
death.

—Genesis 27:2 nkjv

Plan for the golden years. You may get to
experience them.

—Unknown

*Golden years* must have been coined by the young. It is doubt-
ful that anyone over seventy would have described this phase
of life with such a symbolic word. Perhaps a compassionate soul
kindly slipped a *g* in front of the word *old* to ease the ache of reality. After all, the thought of gold brings many grand, but illusive,
ideas to mind. "Invest in gold" is a popular advertisement seen
on television today. "The golden rule" is encouraged by many

but practiced by few, while those who actually demonstrate it also believe that "silence is golden."

So why are the golden years attributed to the aged? Perhaps it's because couples who are fortunate to reach their golden anniversary of fifty years are often seventy or older. I remember when Ruth and I celebrated our golden anniversary in 1993. She was quite proud that she could still slip into the wedding gown she had made as a young bride. I was just proud to still be standing beside her.

The Bible first mentions gold in its description of the lands surrounding Eden (Genesis 2:11–12). No metal in Scripture is mentioned more than gold, and God says it "is mine" (Haggai 2:8). Though it was highly valued, it was used abundantly: from cups to crowns, from shields to bells, from vessels to scepters, from altars to thrones, from door hinges to streets. The Bible speaks of choice gold, precious gold, fine gold, perfect gold, threads of gold, weights of gold, talents of gold, pure gold, dust of gold, cherubim of gold, and even mice of gold (1 Samuel 6:18 NASB). But gold wasn't used just for divine purposes. Men also melted the precious metal to form idols, gods to their own liking. They unwisely valued gold more than God.

Scripture teaches that virtues such as wisdom, knowledge, reputation, and faith are valued more than gold:

> I, wisdom, dwell with prudence,
> And find out knowledge and discretion. . . .
> Counsel is mine, and sound wisdom;
> I am understanding, I have strength. . . .

And those who seek me diligently will find me.

Riches and honor are with me,

Enduring riches and righteousness.

My fruit is better than gold,

    yes, than fine gold. (Proverbs 8:12, 14, 17–19 NKJV)

Here we see the Lord placing a higher value on the virtues of wisdom, knowledge, a good name, and faith. They are just a few of the many attributes of God, and He offers them to those who live for Him. "All the things one may desire cannot be compared with [wisdom]" (Proverbs 8:11 NKJV). In Proverbs 16:16 we are told that it is "much better to get wisdom than gold!" "There is gold and a multitude of rubies, but the lips of knowledge are a precious jewel" (Proverbs 20:15 NKJV).

A good name is to be chosen rather than great riches,

Loving favor rather than silver and gold.

The rich and the poor have this in common,

The LORD is the maker of them all. (Proverbs 22:1–2 NKJV)

Faith is more precious than gold (1 Peter 1:7).

## PLANNING FOR THE FUTURE

You may be asking, "What does this have to do with planning for old age?" The things we value during the prime of life will follow us into the twilight years. If we wisely value faith in the Lord Jesus Christ, it will strengthen us as we age. If we cherish our families by giving them love and understanding, we will likely benefit from continued fellowship with them. When we practice the golden rule, loving others as ourselves, we please God.

Shortly before the economic downturn in 2008, a successful businessman in his forties proudly announced his stock earnings to the tune of several million dollars. "It's been a thrill to see my dream come true," he said. Sometime later, it was reported that his wife had left him and his teenage son, who had spent his lucrative allowances to buy alcohol and drugs, ended up in prison. Many invest wisely in business matters, but fail to invest time and interest in their most valued possessions: their spouses and children.

This is certainly not the case with all those who have successful careers, but the story should serve as a caution. There is a lot to think about at every stage of life. We try to teach our young people to plan for their futures by doing well in school and taking advantage of opportunities to build a strong foundation for adulthood. Parents work hard to provide college educations for their children. Couples try to make wise investments for future retirement. Even senior citizens today are blazing new trails in planning for old age because the golden rules for the golden aged have been drastically altered in recent years.

Because of the tumbling stock market, everyone's nest eggs have lost significant value. Those on the brink of retirement have had to reconsider the dependability of their pensions, 401(k)s, and mutual funds, and in many cases have suddenly changed directions. Nevertheless, planning for retirement and preparing for death have become big businesses, and there is great wisdom in responsibly caring for predictable details.

In Genesis 27, we see Israel's patriarch, Isaac, preparing for his death. He thinks the end is near, so Isaac intends to give the greatest portion of his property to his older son, Esau, as custom requires. Unfortunately his plan is thwarted by two things: the craftiness of his wife and other son, Jacob, and the failure of Isaac's faculties. He inadvertently blesses Jacob, leaving the rightful heir without an inheritance. What I find intriguing in the passage is that Isaac's concern is really for preparing others, namely, his two sons, for his death; but it doesn't go so well. While there are many lessons to be learned from this biblical account, one is that Isaac is too old to ensure his final wishes are executed properly, and this causes turmoil within the family.

While no one likes to dwell on death or prepare for it, the Bible emphasizes these matters. Recently a medical doctor was interviewed about death and financial preparedness on a popular talk radio program. She made a startling statement: "We are not made to experience death. Death is ugly." I wish I could point her to the scripture that says, "Death is swallowed up in victory" (1 Corinthians 15:54 NKJV).

The Bible references death and dying in many ways, nearly one thousand times. Yet the Bible remains a book of great hope. Life stands between bookends: birth and death. Outside of the rapture of the church, there will be one death for every birth. Not everyone will experience old age, but death will come to all. For believers, our hope and comfort come from God's Word, which says, "Blessed are the dead who die in the Lord" (Revelation 14:13 NKJV).

When a child is born, the parents can do nothing to prepare him for "life," for the child already has the breath of life flowing through him. What they must prepare him for are the experiences of life: the disappointments and joys, the defeats and victories, death and everlasting life. What Christian parents do not want their children to understand the cycle of life and the hope of life after death?

As a farm boy, I was exposed to this cycle from my earliest memories. There were lessons to be learned even when a farm animal died. How much more important is the human soul? Many parents today shield their children from anything that may bring sorrow. This has the potential of stunting a child's development and causing emotional trauma. When they become adults, those once-sheltered children cannot cope with the inevitable because they have never been exposed to it. When my golden retriever, Sam, died last year, I remembered how my children used to have funerals when their pets died. It was moving to watch their respect toward death, even for their beloved pets.

Life is uncertain; we don't know what the future may hold. The Bible warns, "Why, you do not even know what will happen tomorrow. What is your life? You are a mist that appears for a little while and then vanishes. . . . Anyone, then, who knows the good he ought to do and doesn't do it, sins" (James 4:14, 17). Since death is an undeniable reality, we should all be diligent to prepare for the last years of life. Things of this nature are serious. I find little humor in making light of such a monumental event, though I admire others who can lighten heavy hearts and bring a twinkle to tear-filled eyes in times of grief.

A family of supporters of our organization told a story about their older sister, who was failing in health. She had no spouse or children, so her siblings were lovingly caring for her in her last days.

They persuaded her to accompany them to see the funeral director. He showed them a number of packages and asked, "Which one is your preference?" The siblings looked at their sister and said, "Which one would you like?" Without changing expression the sister said, "When the time comes, surprise me!" That ended the meeting, and they all returned home with light hearts and the planning complete.

In contrast, an attorney who did not practice what he preached died unexpectedly of a heart attack in his early seventies. For decades people in his community had looked to him for legal advice: transfers of property, disputes between neighbors, family conflicts, wills, and estates—the whole gamut of legal matters a lawyer is often called upon to handle. His clients had confidence in him, not only for his knowledge of the law but also for his practical wisdom and common sense. Even as he scaled back his practice and brought in a younger partner to take over, people still sought him out for advice. Hundreds came to his funeral, and the family was overwhelmed with cards and letters from people he had helped over the years. The local newspaper printed an editorial extolling his contributions to the community and expressing its sense of loss.

Shortly after the funeral, his family made an unsettling—even shocking—discovery: he had never gotten around to preparing his own thorough estate plan. Nor had he informed anyone in his family about his financial affairs; they didn't know what property or securities he owned (if any) or even if he had a safe deposit box. Although from time to time he had expressed a desire to leave some of his estate to his church and to several local charities, as well as to help a widowed sister, in the end none of those verbal wishes were fulfilled. It took many months (and much expense) to sort out his affairs, and it all could have been prevented if he'd only done what he had advised countless others to do over the years: prepare a comprehensive estate plan. Why he never got around to doing this or helping his family understand his financial situation, no one knows. Perhaps—like many—he couldn't quite face the fact that he was getting older and that someday he would die.

Whether it is the question of making a will or one of a dozen other practical issues, growing older confronts us with a number of challenges. If we don't take care of these necessary details, others will step in, possibly creating difficulty for those we have left behind. It is our duty to be responsible for handling matters that affect us individually long after we are gone.

Not every decision can be made in advance, of course; some practical issues can be dealt with only as they occur. No one can predict, for example, if a spouse is going to break a hip or retirement savings are going to shrink because of stock market reversals, much less plan in advance exactly how we will deal with either situation. But some issues can be decided in advance, and when that is the case, we need to take action. God does not want us to leave a legacy of resentment or conflict or confusion behind us, but this can easily happen if we neglect the practical issues that press upon us as we grow older. Remember that "a prudent man gives thought to his steps" (Proverbs 14:15), and "everything should be done in a fitting and orderly way" (1 Corinthians 14:40).

The older we get, the harder it becomes to deal with sensitive issues and important decisions that confront us. They may be too burdensome or complicated for us to sort out at that stage of our lives, or perhaps we would rather avoid potential conflicts and tensions that may arise with others. They also may trigger worrisome thoughts about the inevitable march of time or even make us question our own ability to make sound decisions as we grow older. In addition, the stress of an unexpected illness or the death of a spouse or some other crisis may preoccupy us so much that we are incapable of focusing on other issues. Many older people, doctors tell us, also battle with depression, and a common characteristic of someone who suffers from depression is an inability to make decisions. During trying times, I would encourage you to seek professional advice while considering several matters. My hope is that as you read through these pages you will be encouraged to follow through on them—both for you and those you love.

## MASTERING YOUR MONEY

"I've never met an older person," an attorney told a friend of mine recently, "who didn't worry about their money and whether or not they'll have enough to last them until the end of their days. Even people who have no reason to worry still do."

Our society places too much emphasis on money, implying that financial achievement is the main measure of a person's true success in life. But this is a false standard, and we must resist falling into the trap of thinking that money is everything. Jesus warned, "No one can serve two masters. Either you will hate the one and love the other, or you will be devoted to the one and despise the other. You cannot serve both God and money" (Luke 16:13). Paul later advised his protégé, "People who want to get rich fall into temptation and a trap and into many foolish and harmful desires that plunge men into ruin and destruction. For the love of money is a root of all kinds of evil" (1 Timothy 6:9–10).

Does this mean it is wrong to think about money or do careful financial planning for our latter years? No, of course not. Just make sure that money is your servant and not your master. Does it rule you, or do you rule it? No matter how little or how much you have in the way of financial resources, God has given them to you, and He wants you to be a faithful steward or trustee of them. See your money as a God-given responsibility, not as something you are free to use (or misuse) as you please.

This is especially important as we enter our retirement years because our income then will probably be less (even significantly less) than it has been. "We never bothered making out a budget," someone said. "My wife and I both had good jobs, and we always had enough to do most anything we wanted to do. But suddenly I've realized it isn't true anymore. For the first time in my life, I'm having to watch every penny. I wish I'd done it sooner."

A retiree wrote, "One of the problems of retirement is that it gives you more time to read about the problems of retirement." While the thought is humorous, it is also truthful. But instead of reading about the problems, we should take appropriate action to solve the problems.

What guidelines about money should we follow as we look toward our senior years? What problems do we need to think through, and what decisions should we make before they become a problem? Let me suggest three general guidelines.

*Plan Realistically for Your Retirement*

Numerous websites and other resources can help you calculate how much you will need to save in order to have a comfortable retirement—and yet far too many people never do this, and they end up setting aside very little. Sometimes it is not possible to save for retirement; I think of the letters I receive from single parents or unemployed people who simply cannot set aside anything.

But for those who can, saving money takes discipline. Take full advantage of your company's retirement plan (if it has one), and borrow from it only in an extreme emergency. Many companies also provide ways to deposit part of each paycheck automatically into a savings account. Some companies even match employee contributions to a retirement plan. "Pay yourself first" is an old adage that can serve you well. The Bible's picturesque example of the ant that diligently sets aside food for the future illustrates a practical but profound lesson:

> Go to the ant, you sluggard;
>> consider its ways and be wise! . . .
> It stores its provisions in summer
>> and gathers its food at harvest. (Proverbs 6:6, 8)

I have heard it said, and I wholeheartedly agree that as in all successful ventures, the foundation of a good retirement is planning. I would add to that the necessity of prayer. The Bible tells us to pray about everything, so pray that God will take possession of your life totally and completely. When we do this, we reveal our dependence upon Him.

*Avoid the Traps of Unnecessary Expenditures*

One of the most common financial snares affecting some people as they grow older is what we might call the *debt trap*. The temptation to run up huge credit card bills in order to pay for things we cannot afford (and probably don't need) can happen at any stage of life, but it is especially disastrous for seniors who have no employment income to pay back the debt. Sadly, the debt trap causes some seniors to declare bankruptcy.

Don't give gifts you can't afford. This often happens when grandparents try to buy the affection of children or grandchildren by showering them with overly generous gifts. Harsh as it may sound, some parents use money almost as a weapon, attempting to control their children with it or using it to try to bridge the gap between them and an alienated child. They have forgotten the Bible's wise words: "Above all, love each other deeply, because love covers over a multitude of sins" (1 Peter 4:8).

Guard against unwise financial decisions as you grow older. There are many trustworthy financial planners, but some target older people who may be duped by glowing promises and persuasive presentations. Don't believe everything you hear, and don't make major financial decisions without consulting knowledgeable people you trust. The old adage is right: if it sounds too good to be true, it probably is.

While caution is necessary when considering how to allocate your resources, don't become obsessed about your finances. "All my aunt ever thinks about is her money and her fears that she's going to be left destitute," I heard one man say. "She won't even let me change some burned-out light bulbs because she's afraid she won't be able to afford her electric bill. I know she has more than enough to see her through, but she refuses to believe it, and she's become a prisoner to her fears." Take control of your finances by setting up a sensible budget and sticking to it. This way you won't be a slave to debt, a victim of predators, or a prisoner of fear.

## Deal Frankly with Any Legal Issues

Having a valid will is critically important. Some people avoid doing it because they fear the expense; others feel they don't have enough to make a will worthwhile; still others worry about conflicts a will may cause in their family.

Consider, though, the impact of leaving this world without a will. The implications to your family can be devastating. Laws differ from state to state, but in certain circumstances the fate of the possessions of someone who dies without a will is decided by the courts or by state law, not by the person's family. The result is often much different from what the deceased would have wished. Apart from that, the lack of a will may cause bickering and conflicts between family members who think they are entitled to get certain things from the estate. "Our mother had some nice things," one woman wrote me recently, "but after she died the arguing over who would get what became very bitter. I know she would've been shocked at the way some family members acted. Why are people so greedy? Most of it wasn't worth much anyway." In her letter she mentioned that her mother had died without a will.

Deciding to have a will prepared is only the first step, however; more important are questions about your wishes for the disposal of your property—in other words, who will benefit from your will? But other questions may also need to be addressed as you make your will, such as who the executor of the estate will be, and whether any part of the estate will be placed in trust instead of given outright to an heir. These can be complicated questions with far-reaching implications, and they are best handled with the help of an attorney who is skilled in estate matters.

No matter how simple or complex a person's estate may be, however, any estate plan needs to be prepared thoughtfully, carefully—and prayerfully. God is just as concerned about what you are going to do with your possessions after your death as He is with what you are doing with them right now. Do you see them as yours alone, to be used selfishly and in any way you want, or do you realize they have been entrusted to you by God and are to be used for His glory? A man who has always made a point of tithing his income, of giving one-tenth of it to his church and other Christian organizations, told his family he plans to do the same with his estate, and he has written it into his will. Certainly these written instructions can help clarify the wishes of the deceased. King David prayed, "But who am I, and who are my people, that we should be able to give as generously as this? Everything comes from you, and we have given you only what comes from your hand" (1 Chronicles 29:14).

## LIVING ILL AND LIVING WILL

Most people are familiar with a "last will and testament," a legal document that outlines what they wish to happen after their deaths. In recent years, due to enormous changes within our nation's health care system, an important document has emerged that gives patients certain rights. This is popularly known as a "living will." (This may go by various names, such as an "advance medical directive" or a "declaration of a desire for a natural death.") This document expresses what a person wishes to happen before his or her death—specifically, what the person wishes to happen in case of a physical or mental disability or a major medical emergency. Living wills have become important mainly because of medical advances that can prolong a person's life well beyond its normal expectancy, even in dire circumstances.

Closely associated with the living will may be other types of legal documents, such as powers of attorney that authorize another person to act on your behalf in case you are unable to function on your own. A "health care power of attorney" allows you to designate a family member or other trusted person to make medical decisions concerning your care if you are no longer able to make them for yourself. Similarly, a "financial power of attorney" designates someone who can make financial decisions on your behalf in case of your incapacity. Always be careful about signing any document of this nature under pressure (such as when undergoing emergency medical care in another state) to be sure it doesn't change your true wishes or reverse something you signed previously.

These are difficult, complex, and emotional issues to decide; but when the medical consensus is that there is no reasonable hope of recovery, my own conviction is that extreme measures are only artificially delaying a person's death, not prolonging life. As much as possible, such matters need to be decided before they become necessary and then set forth in a valid legal document. Once a medical emergency develops, it is usually impossible for the patient to express his wishes in a way that will give clear and legal guidance to the doctor or hospital. Incidentally, many hospitals now have on their websites suggested forms to deal with these matters.

Why go to the trouble of having a living will or any other document that comes into effect only when you are unable to function on your own? The most obvious reason is to spare yourself what might otherwise be a prolonged period of suffering and indignity when there is, in fact, no hope of recovery. But a living will is also important for the same reason your last will and testament is important: for the sake of your family. Lacking any directive from you, family members may find themselves caught in a confusing and emotional web of difficult choices—and they may not all agree on the way forward. In addition, laws in some states (so I understand) may mandate extreme measures that cannot be withdrawn once they are started. The expense and the emotional toll on the family can be staggering—but more than that, in such situations the true wishes of the patient will be ignored because they were never put in writing. Help yourself and your family avoid what can become a nightmare.

Christians are not to be preoccupied with death; God has put within each of us a will to survive. But neither are we to shrink from death or act as if we must fiercely resist it until the last breath. The time may well come, in fact, when life's burdens and pains overwhelm us so much that we will welcome death as a friend—and that is as it should be. If we know Christ, we know that Heaven is our true home, and (like the saints of old) we are "longing for a better country—a heavenly one" (Hebrews 11:16).

## A WORD TO ADULT CHILDREN

Remember that one day everyone will be facing old age. I can recall as a young adult worrying about my parents as they aged. I always tried to give them the respect they earned and deserved, and I was cautious not to insult them by suggesting that they could no longer make important decisions about their lives. A fine line sometimes separates preserving your parents' dignity and ensuring their well-being.

Perhaps some may be saying, "Well, I'm sure those things are important, but I'm still young, and all this seems a long way off for me." You are probably right; but your parents may be in turmoil about how their decisions affect not only them but you.

Some adult children worry that their parents are not taking these steps, and the children are reluctant to bring it up, thinking that the parents may mistake their motives. This does present a problem sometimes. The relationship between parents and their adult children can be difficult. As a rule adults don't like to be told what to do by their parents—and parents don't like to be told what to do by their children. But refusing to act on the practical issues that confront us as we grow older (or simply ignoring them) often becomes a sure recipe for turmoil and conflict within a family. I encourage adult children to consider turning the tables. Ask your parents' advice as you seek what plans you should also put in place. Perhaps this would open up the discussion because, after all, they may also be reluctant to bring up dreaded subjects. Sometimes older people need their children's perspective—and perhaps this approach can be the nudge that is needed.

Only you know the dynamics within your own family, but I encourage you not to draw back from trying to help in these important matters. Ask the Lord to give you wise words and a sense of right timing for such discussions. The Lord honors His people who do all in His name with respect, gentleness, and love. Take to heart the Bible's admonition: "The wisdom that comes from heaven is first of all pure; then peace-loving, considerate, submissive, full of mercy and good fruit, impartial and sincere" (James 3:17).

## A WORD TO PARENTS

My prayer is that you will be responsible for settling the business that must take place when living wills and last wills and final arrangements must be made. It is emotionally hard on others to make such decisions for a loved one. Be proactive so others won't have to be reactive. The older generation should set an example of making important decisions while they are able to do so. Your children will someday be dealing with the same issues you are today. You can bless your children with the example of responsible planning.

I remember being moved when I read the last will and testament of the late J. P. Morgan. He is noted as perhaps the most influential banker in history. I have often wondered about the reaction of his children when they read their father's will after his death in 1913. I hope they sensed the power of his words and gained strength from them: "I commit my soul into the hands of my Saviour, in full confidence that having redeemed it and washed it in His most precious blood He will present it faultless before the throne of my Heavenly Father; and I entreat my children to maintain and defend, at all hazard, and at any cost of personal sacrifice, the blessed doctrine of the complete atonement for sin through the blood of Jesus Christ, once offered, and through that alone."[1]

Making choices for ourselves is not easy, but leaving them to someone else is risky. Having your house in order is one of the most important things parents can do for their children. Give them the *peace of mind* that you have your *piece of mind* and have taken care of the business that has come about from your lifetime of labor. More than anything else, let them know where you stand with the Lord Jesus Christ, for this will be your lasting legacy.

## NEARING HOME WITH RESPONSIBLE PLANNING

Are we joyfully giving thanks in all circumstances, or are we making our last years on earth unbearable for ourselves and those close to us? Are we obediently setting things in place so that others will know that we were responsible followers of Christ? Are we preparing for death with the assurance that Jesus is preparing our homecoming? When we reach our destiny, will others know where we are?

The book of Hebrews has a lot to say about wills and testaments: "In the case of a will, it is necessary to prove the death of the one who made it, because a will is in force only when somebody has died; it never takes effect while the one who made it is living" (Hebrews 9:16–17). Jesus came and dwelt among mankind. He was the example of how to live—and how to die. He came to die so that we may live. He also was resurrected in order to fulfill the promise He made: "I go to prepare a place for you" (John 14:2 NKJV). This is why the Bible says, "Precious in the sight of the LORD is the death of his saints" (Psalm 116:15). This is a wonderful last will and testament. We may grow impatient with our circumstances in our remaining years of life, but as we wait for the reunion with our Savior, let's recall *God's will* for us: "Be joyful always; . . . give thanks in all circumstances, for this is *God's will* for you in Christ Jesus" (1 Thessalonians 5:16–18, emphasis added).

# 5 FADING STRENGTH BUT STANDING STRONG

Do not cast me off in the time of old age;
Do not forsake me when my strength fails.

—Psalm 71:9 NKJV

Stand up to your obstacles. You will find that they
haven't half the strength you think they have.

—Norman Vincent Peale

The headline of an article that appeared in 2010 on a Tokyo website stated, "A robot suit that gives super strength to the elderly." Included was a picture of the power suit modeled not by a senior adult but by an athletic youth. The caption stated that the heavy-duty suit weighs sixty-six pounds and will be originally priced at 1 million yen (approximately $12,000). I asked myself, "How many my age have the strength to carry around sixty-six pounds for an hour, much less all day; and who could possibly afford such an expense?" I was relieved that the article indicated that there were no plans to sell the suits overseas. I'll just be content struggling to get my shoes on each morning!

I had to look carefully at the article to discern just how an exoskeleton suit made of metal and plastic could give any strength. The secret was not in the suit but in the eight electric motors and sensors responding to commands through a voice-recognition system, enabling the body to lift and bend without strain to the muscles. While this futuristic invention may never be seen in our department stores, the brainstorming behind it reveals man's desire for strength and power beyond himself.

A sixty-five-year-old father was helping his son move into a new house. When the son told his buddies about it, he said, "Dad and I were trying to move the freezer into the kitchen. I went to the garage to get the hand truck. When I returned, my dad had moved the freezer across the deck and into the kitchen the hard way—by sheer strength! My first response was to remind him he could have thrown his back out or pulled a muscle. Then I saw the twinkle in his eye. He was proud of his accomplishment, and I have to say, I was proud of him. *Old man strength* came to mind, and I concluded that there was a lot I could learn from this man with the silver hair who has always stood strong and exhibited sheer determination."

The Bible says, "The glory of young men is their strength, and the splendor of old men is their gray head" (Proverbs 20:29 NKJV). Young people often take for granted the strength and wisdom the aged can still possess, and the aged sometimes push the limits of their wisdom! But I can certainly remember as a young man thinking of my father as one with great strength. He was a farmer. He worked with his hands. And as he grew older, my respect grew deeper for his strength of wisdom.

As I am living much longer than my father did, one of my great surprises in the aging process has been the loss of strength to do the simplest things: getting up from a chair, having endurance to visit with someone longer than an hour, or just going to the doctor's office. God knows our infirmities. He knows our strength wanes as the years pass. Our dependence on Him delights Him. Paul reminds us in Colossians 1:29 that he depended on Christ's mighty power that works within, and we can claim this as well. Remember, He didn't create our bodies to live forever, and He knows exactly how we feel.

We shouldn't spend time thinking about ourselves and how weak we are. Instead we should think about God and how strong He is. Just as the sensors built into the power suit respond by voice recognition and infuse the suit with power, we are told to respond to God's voice and He will be our strength. The psalmist wrote, "My flesh and my heart fail; but God is the strength of my heart" (Psalm 73:26 NKJV). Are we depending on Him? Are we recognizing His voice?

## WHEN GOD SPEAKS

I have never heard the voice of the Lord audibly, but the Lord has spoken to me many times throughout my life. You might ask, "How can someone recognize His voice?" The Bible says, "Everyone who is of the truth hears My voice" (John 18:37 NKJV). To recognize the voice of the Lord, we must belong to Him.

A grandmother and granddaughter were shopping together one day, and every time the young girl's mobile phone would ring, she would immediately answer by saying the caller's name. After several phone calls, the grandmother was puzzled and asked, "Dear, how is it that you know the name of the person before they even have a chance to speak?" The granddaughter giggled, hugged her grandmother's neck, and said, "It's a new technology, Granny. Caller ID." When the granddaughter explained how it worked, the grandmother said, "Well, I declare, we didn't have to have that technology back in my day. My neighbor was the one who identified all those who called—we shared a party line." Then the granddaughter was the one perplexed until she heard the amazing story of shared phone lines, before her time.

Well, Ruth never had to identify herself when she called me on my many trips around the world. When I picked up the phone and heard her speak, I knew the voice of my wife. That was also years before mobile phones and caller ID. I never had to ask my children to identify themselves by name when they phoned. I could easily distinguish the voices of my daughters Gigi, Anne, and Bunny, and my two sons Franklin and Ned. My sisters Catherine and Jean, and my brother, Melvin, were unmistakable voices to me. I can remember times when I would answer the phone and hear my mother's sweet voice. I never had to ask who was calling. We recognize the voices of those who are dear to us and those with whom we commune.

Likewise, if we are communicating with the Lord Jesus through prayer and meditating on His Word, our spirits will identify with His voice. Jesus said, "My sheep hear My voice, and I know them, and they follow Me" (John 10:27 NKJV). The Lord would not expect us to hear His voice if He did not make it possible. He sends out His mighty voice (Psalm 68:33) and says we can hear it (Psalm 95:7): "I will give them hearts that recognize me as the LORD" (Jeremiah 24:7 NLT); and "Obey My voice, and I will be your God" (Jeremiah 7:23 NKJV).

The voice of the Lord comes in various ways: a voice in the midst of the fire (Deuteronomy 5:24); a voice upon the waters (Psalm 29:3); a voice from Heaven (Matthew 3:17); a voice out of the cloud (Matthew 17:5); the voice of His mouth (Acts 22:14); a voice from the excellent glory (2 Peter 1:17); and a voice out of the throne (Revelation 19:5).

Do we listen for His voice in our everyday activity? Sometimes He speaks, but we don't hear. We can't blame it on the batteries going dead in our hearing aids. God's voice is not bound by man's inventions. God speaks to the human heart. His voice is described as full of majesty (Psalm 29:4), a still small voice (1 Kings 19:12), and a glorious voice (Isaiah 30:30). The Lord's voice is identified as the voice of the living God (Deuteronomy 5:26), the voice of the bridegroom (Jeremiah 7:34), and the voice of the Almighty (Ezekiel 1:24).

His is a powerful voice (Psalm 29:4). It shakes the wilderness (Psalm 29:8), divides the flames of fire (Psalm 29:7), thunders (Job 37:5), and rushes like many waters (Revelation 1:15); and His voice cries to the city (Micah 6:9). We are to obey His voice (Deuteronomy 13:4) and hearken to the voice of His word (Psalm 103:20).

Telecommunications have changed our world. It used to be that when I would get on an airplane, my wife would be assured she wouldn't hear from me for hours. Now there are few instances when anyone is disconnected. We can call from the sky while in flight. It is no longer necessary to pull off the highway to make a call from a pay phone. But sometimes reception is difficult. It is not unusual for a cellular phone to drop a call in midsentence or for the transmission to be interrupted momentarily because of interference. Often people nearly scream into the phone, "Can you hear me?" A reply comes back, "I can hear you. Can you hear me?" It's sometimes comical to hear the younger generation ask their peers to repeat themselves.

The first question God asked man is: "Where are you?" Adam answered, "I heard Your voice in the garden" (Genesis 3:9–10 NKJV). God also questioned the woman, "What is this you have done?" (Genesis 3:13 NKJV). If Eve had had a mobile phone, she may have suggested there was interference on the line.

But there is nothing humorous about broken communication with the Lord of our lives. When it happens, I can assure you that we are the interference—not Him. Sometimes we don't want to hear what He has to say because we already know what the Word of God has told us. The Bible is full of accounts of men and women hearing the voice of the Lord but not recognizing it at first. This happened to the prophet Samuel. God called him by name, over and over. Samuel thought it was someone else. But the Lord persisted until Samuel recognized His voice (1 Samuel 3:11).

If God did not want to commune with us, then He would not question man; but not only does He want to communicate *with* us, He also wants to hear *from* us. He expects a response. Isaiah "heard the voice of the Lord saying, 'Whom shall I send?'" Isaiah responded, "Here am I. Send me!" (Isaiah 6:8). The persecutor of Christians heard the voice of the Lord saying, "Saul, Saul, why are you persecuting Me?" In this remarkable exchange, Saul responded, "Who are You, Lord? . . . What do You want me to do?" (Acts 9:4–6 NKJV). This dialogue was the beginning of the apostle Paul's great ministry.

But God's voice isn't always heard in the form of a question. He is a loving God who cares about our needs. His voice gives comfort and guidance. Gideon heard the Lord speak peace (Judges 6:23), and Habakkuk heard God's voice say, "The righteous will live by his faith" (Habakkuk 2:4).

Many people have told me over the years that they believe God speaks through His Word, but they don't believe He actually hears their pleas. Scripture dispels this. For those who fear and honor the Lord, He hears the voice of weeping (Psalm 6:8) and says,

> Refrain your voice from weeping,
> And your eyes from tears;
> For your work shall be rewarded. . . .
> There is hope in your future. (Jeremiah 31:16–17 NKJV)

If ever you feel lonely and weak, listen for God's words of comfort: "Hear my voice" (Isaiah 28:23), and "Lift up your voice with strength" (Isaiah 40:9 NKJV). He hears the voice of your words (Deuteronomy 5:28) and attends to your voice in prayer (Psalm 66:19). I hope these reminders from Scripture boost your spirit.

At my age I can sympathize with most seniors. The good old days call me back at times, especially when I am with friends who have shared so much. While I choose not to dwell on the past or relive my youth, there are times I long to hike up into the hills with my children or stand in the pulpit to deliver a Gospel message. But the walker, wheelchair, and cane near my bed remind me that chapter in life is past. So I thank God for the memories that have enriched my life but look forward to new opportunities, to experiences that can add some dimension to the present. Our attitudes play a major role in the closing scene on life's stage.

## WHEN YOUTH FADES

"Birthdays are good for you," someone said. "Statistics show that the people who have the most live the longest." A reply came, "Looking fifty is great—if you are sixty!" It is all perspective. Children look at their thirty-year-old parents as old, their grandparents as ancient. Grandparents look at their children and grandchildren as forever young. Yet children are always pushing their young age up as fast as they can. Ask a child how old he or she is. The answer will always end with "and a half." A ten-year-old can't wait to be twelve. The twelve-year-old wants to be a teenager. The teenager wants to be old enough to get married. Couples are anxious to marry their children off so they can become grandparents. When they get to the grandparent stage, they begin complaining about being too old.

Our society is made up of obsessive contradictions: the young want to be rewarded with big jobs without obtaining experience, the middle-aged brag about working out at the gym but can't wait to retire in order to rest, and the old want to drink from the fountain of youth. The truth is that instant success robs young people of the journey; but it is along the journey that we obtain knowledge, collect memories, and have a sense of achievement that makes life a rewarding experience. And older people are often deceived by miracle drugs and creams promising renewed beauty and vigor. Juan Ponce de León, the Spanish explorer who traveled at one time with Christopher Columbus, went in search of a magic water source that people called the Fountain of Youth. Rumor had it that drinking its waters would keep one young. Ponce de León was determined to find this legendary fountain; instead he found Florida—what became America's retirement haven. How many couples have packed their belongings, pulled up roots, and left home and family to set up housekeeping in a condo on a Florida golf course—with a nursing home across the fairway?

A plastic surgeon in the Sunshine State named his private practice Fountain of Youth Institute, but according to a recent report by *Scientific American*, the Fountain of Youth is a myth. It reports, "The prospect of immortality has always had universal appeal." The article includes a position statement containing this warning: "No currently marketed intervention—none—has yet been proved to slow, stop or reverse human aging."[1]

I am reminded of a young teenager who pulled up a chair beside his grandfather and said, "Poppy, the wrinkles on your face are starting to cover up the scar you are so proud of!" The wise grandfather smiled, patted the boy on the back, and said, "Son, scars, wrinkles, and rusty bones have lots of stories to tell." That afternoon, the grandson learned about his heritage. A few years later, he enlisted in the United States military. When asked why, he replied, "I want to earn my scars and wrinkles like my grandfather did."

The world's idea of a fountain of youth is a mirage. Only the Bible provides an oasis for the soul: "The fear of the LORD is a fountain of life" (Proverbs 14:27). To grasp the meaning of this verse, we must first understand what "fear of the LORD" means. It is contrary to being afraid of Him. God would not have sent His Son to earth to communicate with us if He wanted humanity to be fearful of approaching Him. This wonderful phrase throughout Scripture is a reminder to be in reverential awe of God, to love Him with our whole being and commit ourselves joyfully to Him in all things: "Love the LORD your God with all your heart, with all your soul, and with all your strength" (Deuteronomy 6:5 NKJV). The apostle John said it this way: "Keep away from anything that might take God's place in your hearts" (1 John 5:21 NLT).

Here we see a wonderful picture of a fountain that flows with life-giving blessings: "For you are the fountain of life, the light by which we see" (Psalm 36:9 NLT); "The words of the godly are a life-giving fountain" (Proverbs 10:11 NLT); "The instruction of the wise is like a life-giving fountain" (Proverbs 13:14 NLT); and "Discretion is a life-giving fountain" (Proverbs 16:22 NLT). Then the Lord Jesus sums it all up in the closing book of the Bible: "I am the Alpha and the Omega, the Beginning and the End. I will give of the fountain of the water of life freely to him who thirsts. He who overcomes shall inherit all things" (Revelation 21:6–7 NKJV).

The fountain of life is real, friends. We can draw strength from its resources and stand strong in our resolve to be overcomers, looking forward to the inheritance and being in the presence of the Savior of our souls. Though the eyes of the tired, overworked, and aged may dim, His light will pour into our hearts. While the lips of the elderly may be silenced, godly words will continue to flow through our beings. When hearing is a challenge, wise instruction can run through our innermost thoughts. While many may lose their ability to make decisions, others will benefit from their experiences as they also blaze new trails.

Some time ago I met an acquaintance I hadn't seen for at least twenty-five years. As we shook hands the thought flashed through my mind, *My goodness, he's turned into an old man!* (He probably thought the same about me.) When I had last seen him, he was tall and athletic; now he was stooped and wrinkled, trembling slightly and leaning heavily on his cane. He was still the same person, but the years had taken their toll.

Later it occurred to me that if we had seen each other every few months instead of only once in twenty-five years, we'd probably not have noticed any changes. As a rule growing older is an extended, gradual process; we don't go to bed young one night and suddenly wake up old the next day. Just as life is a journey of many steps, so is that part we commonly call the golden years. And yet if we live long enough, old age inevitably will overtake us.

We may not like to admit this; we may even deny it and devote our energies to keeping old age at bay. Cosmetic companies and plastic surgeons promise to keep us looking youthful if we will only use their products or submit to their services;

vitamin manufacturers claim their wares can retard the aging process; exercise gurus and medical experts point to the benefits of healthy living. Up to a point some of their claims may be valid. Careful attention to our health may slow down the aging process and ward off some of its more onerous effects—at least for a time. This isn't necessarily wrong; God wants us to take care of our bodies. The Bible says, "Honor God with your body" (1 Corinthians 6:20).

In reality some people seem to have stronger genes and age more slowly than others. Some are old at sixty; others seem almost ageless. As I dictate this, my longtime associate and friend George Beverly Shea has just celebrated his 102nd birthday, and he is still alert and sprightly. Several months ago he spent a couple of days sharing his music with prisoners at Louisiana State Penitentiary in Angola, Louisiana, one of our nation's largest prisons. Shortly after his birthday he and his wife, Karlene, journeyed to Hollywood, where he was honored with a lifetime Grammy Award for his singing career—the oldest person ever to receive that prestigious (and well-deserved) honor.

Within days of Bev's return, he and Cliff Barrows, who has served with me in ministry from the beginning, participated in one of Bill Gaither's Homecoming videos taped at the Billy Graham Library. The outdoor concert was taped under an enormous tent with 140 Gospel music artists on the platform. Cliff at age 88 and Bev at age 102 sat on stage singing with the others the great songs of faith way into the night. When Bill and Gloria Gaither came to my home for a visit the next day, they told me how Cliff walked to the center of the platform and led the great choir and congregation in singing "Blessed Assurance." Others reported to me that in spite of Cliff's cane, he directed that night with "gusto." I have seen Cliff lead hundreds of massive choirs down through the years, but I would have liked to have been there.

But no matter who you are, nothing will halt the onset of old age completely, and like it or not, the longer you live the more its burdens and disabilities will become your companions. Rather than deny the realities and ravages of old age, it is far better to admit them and prepare for them—and, by God's grace, even welcome them as part of His plan for life.

## WHEN LIFE SLOWS DOWN

If I had to summarize in one word the changes that come over us as we grow older, I'd probably have to use the word *decline*. Most obvious is the decline in physical strength and the ability to do everything we once did. Gradually our muscles grow stiff and lose strength; our mobility lessens; our hearing and eyesight begin to deteriorate; our reactions slow down; our physical stamina begins to fade. Much as I might wish otherwise, at the age of ninety-two I no longer can get out of a chair by myself. Several years ago my doctors insisted I begin using a walker to prevent me from losing my balance and falling. I would have been foolish to ignore their warning.

As age increases, energy decreases. Everything seems to take longer, even recovering from illness or periods of activity. Someone asked me once what my biggest surprise was about growing older, and after thinking about it, I answered, "The loss of strength, the sheer inability to keep going." In a weakened state, disability and pain are unwelcome guests that not only refuse to leave but also threaten to move in and take over.

Another new reality in this stage of life is watching friends and family members become ill or die. Hardly a week goes by without news reaching me about the illness or death of someone I have known. But it's not only the aged. It seems as though more and more young people are being diagnosed with diseases that once were thought diseases for the elderly. Parkinson's disease has attacked many young bodies, and I have known many parents who have taken a grown child back into the home to care for him.

In some cases older folks can learn from the younger who are dealt such blows. One young man comes to mind. He was in the prime of life—thirty years old—and had an exciting future planned. As he was driving down a highway, a pain in his chest caused him to pull over at the side of the road. When the worst of the pain subsided, he drove himself to the hospital and within days was diagnosed with a malignant tumor wrapped around his heart. Through months of surgery and treatment, his attitude amazed the doctors at the University of Michigan. He was a good-looking young man. In spite of the tubes, needles, and strong medications, his countenance shined. When the doctors asked him where he drew his strength from, he was able to share Christ with them. While the doctors gave him little hope, they tried to encourage him by saying that a miracle could save his life. He looked at them with blessed assurance and said, "Docs, I'm in a win-win play-off. If I live I win. If I die I win." Not long after, he passed away with the great assurance that he would be united with the Lord, and he left behind a testimony that is still remembered at the University of Michigan Medical Center. That's a lesson from which we all can learn.

There is no doubt that catastrophic illnesses take their tolls on the elderly. Just as our bodies age and decline, so do our minds. In reality the two are closely connected; as we age, physical changes take place in our brains as well as the rest of our bodies, causing everything from mild memory loss to dementia and Alzheimer's disease.

Alzheimer's is a cruel disease. I still remember the sadness I always felt when visiting former President Reagan, after the disease had tightened its grip on his mind, and he couldn't quite recall either who people were or the office he had once held. I last saw him on the lawn of his home in Bel Air, California, at the invitation of his wife, Nancy. After I visited with her in their living room, she asked if I would like to say hello to Mr. Reagan, and I readily agreed. We stepped outside into the bright California sun. A nurse was helping the former president with his lunch. He didn't seem to notice either Nancy or me as we greeted him. After a short (and one-sided) conversation, Nancy asked me to lead in prayer—something I'd always done whenever I visited them, whether in Washington or California. Afterward, as Nancy was escorting me back to my car, I asked her, "Do you think he knew me?" She responded, "Not until you prayed—but hearing you then, I believe he knew who was praying for him."

I have heard similar stories. An author recently told about watching her father suffer from the effects of dementia. He had not spoken in months and had not called her name. But just before he died, she took his hand and began reciting the Lord's Prayer. He spoke every word with her with clarity.

Watching helplessly as a loved one's memory relentlessly fades must surely be one of life's hardest burdens, and those who endure it deserve our compassion and prayers.

The occasional memory lapse, however, that comes to all of us with age isn't serious; it only reminds us that we aren't as young as we once were. At worst it may be mildly embarrassing; at best it may even be humorous. A few years ago I was being introduced at a reception by the host, a man about my age whom I had known for many years. He was recalling to the group how we had first met through a mutual friend we both knew well. "His name," he announced, "was . . . was . . . oh, it's on the tip of my tongue. I know it as well as I know my own name. It was . . . it was . . ." He finally asked me in exasperation, "Billy—what on earth was his name?" But I had to confess I couldn't think of it either—and we both dissolved in laughter at our aging memories. It calmed our fears when a minute later the name came to us.

## WHEN HIDDEN PERILS COME TO LIGHT

We can see ourselves in many Scripture passages, such as this one:

> You sweep men away in the sleep of death;
> they are like the new grass of the morning—
> though in the morning it springs up new,
> by evening it is dry and withered. (Psalm 90:5–6)

His description is all too realistic, I've discovered; dry and withered are exactly how every older person I have ever met feels at times—including me.

While the physical and mental effects of old age are obvious, aging often impacts us in ways that are less obvious. These are the emotional and spiritual reactions to growing older that can easily overwhelm us if we aren't on the alert for them. And yet, because they aren't as obvious as a broken hip or a lost memory, they often sneak into our lives without us even being aware of them.

What are these hidden perils? Certainly one is fear. When we are facing the uncertainties of illness or growing disability or loneliness or financial stress, it is natural to be worried about what is going to happen to us. But sometimes our worries overwhelm us, and we become so absorbed by them that whatever has caused them becomes all we think about. Instead of having a passing worry, we become gripped by chronic, unrelenting fear and anxiety.

Another hidden peril is often related to fear and anxiety: depression. We look back and think about all the things we have done in life, and now we are discouraged to think we will never do them again. Doctors tell us that depression is one of the most common (and most serious) problems many older people face, although it often goes undetected. Common symptoms such as fatigue, forgetfulness, and feelings of loneliness are easily explained away as effects of aging when they could be treated.

A hidden peril of a different sort is anger. No one likes to lose control over life; we all would like to remain independent as we grow older. But often that is not possible, and this is not easy for us to accept. "I've never seen Mother like this before," one person said to me. "She used to be so gentle, but now she lashes out at me every time I come in her room. I know what's wrong: she hates not being in her own home any longer and having to depend on others to take care of her although there really wasn't any choice." His comment could be echoed by countless others. Sometimes the anger is directed not only at others but also at God: "If God really loved me, He wouldn't have let this happen." A friend commented recently, "People either seem to get better or to get bitter as they grow older." Unfortunately, bitterness often wins.

A further peril may creep up on us as we grow older: intense loneliness, even feelings of abandonment. "No one cares what happens to me," a woman in a nursing home said to me once. "My children live in different parts of the country and seldom come to see me. Often I cry myself to sleep, I feel so alone." My heart went out to her, although I knew that others in her facility were facing similar situations.

Sometimes in their loneliness older people get drawn into making unwise decisions such as marrying someone they barely know or spending large sums of money on things they don't need simply because a salesman acts friendly toward them. Many years ago an aunt of mine lived in Orlando, Florida. She had never married, but in the course of her life she had accumulated a fairly large amount of property. In her latter years, we discovered, a man with a gracious personality befriended her and wormed his way into her confidence. In time he convinced her to sell much of her property and allow him to invest her money for her.

Shortly before she died, she discovered that most of the money had vanished. The man simply had taken advantage of her—and her loneliness.

One final peril is becoming so absorbed in our own problems and concerns that we can't think about anyone else. "No one is more self-centered than a sick person," a nurse told me once after dealing with a particularly difficult patient. I'm afraid she's often right; sometimes I have to force my mind to turn away from whatever problem is absorbing me at the moment and make myself focus on the needs of others. Job had the same problem; in the midst of his pain and grief he apparently forgot the spiritual truths he'd once used to encourage others in their troubles. One of his friends gently rebuked him for this:

> Think how you have instructed many,
>     how you have strengthened feeble hands.
> Your words have supported those who stumbled;
>     you have strengthened faltering knees.
> But now trouble comes to you, and you are discouraged. . . .
> Should not your piety [your devotion to God] be your
>     confidence? (Job 4:3–6)

## WHEN CHRIST IS THE FOCUS

How do we overcome the perils that steal our zest for life? Let the promises of God's Word, the Bible, uphold you every day. Turn constantly to Him in prayer, confident not only that He hears you but that even now Jesus is interceding for you. Focus your thoughts on Christ, and maintain your connection with other believers who can encourage and help you. The Bible's words are true: "Neither death nor life, neither angels nor demons, neither the present nor the future . . . nor anything else in all creation, will be able to separate us from the love of God that is in Christ Jesus our Lord" (Romans 8:38–39).

In the weeks before her death, my wife, Ruth, repeated these verses over and over to us. Ruth was always thinking of others. This was her secret for getting through so much of life with joy. She never focused on her problems, she turned her attention to Christ, and He always led her to someone who needed a word of encouragement or a listening ear.

My sister Catherine was in a nursing home several years before her death. She had restricted mobility, and her health was fragile. But she knew all the residents and patiently listened to their concerns. She showed them the compassion of Christ and had many opportunities to witness. The Lord used her even in her own hours of weakness.

I have been told about an eighty-six-year-old lady who is dealing with debilitating illnesses, yet she goes from church on Sundays to the local nursing home to visit the elderly, read Scripture to them, and pray for them. She looks forward to this each week. She's focused on others.

A ninety-six-year-old grandmother has "lots of time at home alone," she says. "I just sit in my chair and go through my prayer list. My goodness, there are so many people to pray for that it seems I run out of time."

Another lady inching close to one hundred looks forward every week to helping deliver Meals on Wheels "to the old people." She's focused on people.

The Lord blesses people who bless others, and He gives grace to those who focus on the things that please Him.

Life is seldom easy as we grow older, but old age has its special joys—the joy of time with family and friends, the joy of freedom from responsibilities we once had, and the joy of savoring the little things we once overlooked. But most of all, as we learn to trust every day into His hands, the golden years can be a time of growing closer to Christ. And that is life's greatest joy.

## NEARING HOME WITH GOD'S STRENGTH

True joy is derived from depending on the Lord Jesus. He is the One who supplies our strength in weakness, for when we are weak, He is strong (2 Corinthians 12:10). While it is important to put our own house in order, we must not forget to make the things of God the center of our thinking and doing. This was certainly the state of mind for the prophet Haggai, who wrote the second shortest book in the Old Testament at the approximate age of seventy. Haggai was stirred up by the Lord to rebuild the Temple in Jerusalem following the Babylonian captivity. In turn he stirred up God's people by rebuking them for allowing the house of God to remain in ruins in their homeland: "Give careful thought to your ways. . . . You expected much, but see, it turned out to be little. . . . Why? . . . Because of my house, which remains a ruin, while each of you is busy with your own house" (Haggai 1:7–9).

What stirs me about this two-chapter book is Haggai's rebuke along with his encouragement. Haggai mobilized God's people to take care of God's business and build up His house by giving them hope: "Be strong. . . . For I am with you" (Haggai 2:4).

We may be successful in putting our personal affairs in place, but if we do it at the sacrifice of the more important—putting our spiritual affairs in order—we miss the joy and purpose of life. The Bible says, "A wise man is strong, yes, a man of knowledge increases strength" (Proverbs 24:5 NKJV). Strength is found in the wisdom of God, and that is at our disposal whether young or old.

Are you concerned only about taking care of business in a world that holds you captive? Or are you setting Christ at the center of your life with the assurance that you will abide with Him for eternity—the place where hope becomes reality? Your strength may fade, but He is the One who will lift you up and help you stand strong in your weakness. When your faith begins to fade, ask the Lord to stir it up by considering all He has done for you, and be strong, for "My Spirit remains among you; do not fear!" (Haggai 2:5 NKJV).

# 6 DEATH'S DESTINATION

The dead will hear the voice of the Son of God; and
those who hear will live.

—John 5:25 NKJV

I am still in the land of the dying; I shall be in the
land of the living soon.

—John Newton

A headline on an Internet site read, "Death, the nation's #1
killer." The point was obvious—death is inevitable!

No one can outrun death. It will catch up to all of us eventually. When I was interviewed by *Newsweek* in 2006 and asked to give a statement about death, I commented that I had been taught all of my life how to die, but no one had ever taught me how to grow old. That statement triggered a lot of interest, and I began thinking about writing this book.

I am certainly no expert on the subject of growing old, but now that I am gaining some experience, I have to admit that not all things get better with age. I have a newfound appreciation—and understanding—when I read this passage in Ecclesiastes 12:

> Remember now your Creator in the days of your youth,
>     Before the difficult days come, . . .
> Remember your Creator before the silver cord is loosed.
>     (vv. 1, 6 NKJV)

When I read this passage as a young preacher, I can assure you I did not relate to it as I do now. What impresses me now is that Solomon, the wisest king ever to rule Israel, intended for the young to read it "in the days of . . . youth, *before* the difficult days come" (emphasis added).

When I was young, I could not imagine being old. My mother said, and the doctor confirmed, that I had an unusual amount of energy; and it followed me into young adulthood. When middle age set in, I dealt with physical weariness, but my mind was always in high gear, and it never took long for my physical stamina to return after a grueling schedule. It tires me out to dwell on it now, wondering how I ever kept up with such a jam-packed itinerary. I fought growing old in every way. I faithfully exercised and was careful to pace myself as I began to feel the grasp of Old Man Time. This was not a transition that I welcomed, and I began to dread what I knew would follow.

My wife, Ruth, however, was one of those who could lighten heavy hearts, especially mine. I will never forget when she announced what she wanted engraved on her gravestone, and for those who have so respectfully visited her gravesite at the Billy Graham Library, they have noticed that what she planned for was carried out to the letter.

Long before she became bedridden, she was driving along a highway through a construction site. Carefully following the detours and mile-by-mile cautionary signs, she came to the last one that said, "End of Construction. Thank you for your patience." She arrived home, chuckling and telling the family about the posting. "When I die," she said, "I want that engraved on my stone." She was lighthearted but serious about her request. She even wrote it out so that we wouldn't forget. While we found the humor enlightening, we appreciated the truth she conveyed through those few words. Every human being is under construction from conception to death. Each life is made up of mistakes and learning, waiting and growing, practicing patience and being persistent. At the end of construction—death—we have completed the process.

> You formed my inward parts; . . .
> My frame was not hidden from You,
>> When I was made in secret,
>> And skillfully wrought. . . .
> The days fashioned for me. (Psalm 139:13, 15–16 NKJV)

Death says, "This is the finality of accomplishment." While we cannot add anything more to our experience, believers in Christ have the hope of hearing the Savior say, "Well done, good and faithful servant" (Matthew 25:21 NKJV).

The apostle Paul spoke of the Christian being "rooted and built up in Him and established in the faith" (Colossians 2:7 NKJV). This is part of our ongoing construction in this life. But the Bible assures us that "if our earthly house, this tent, is destroyed, we have a building from God, a house not made with hands, eternal in the heavens" (2 Corinthians 5:1 NKJV). When Ruth was separated from her pain-stricken body and earthly construction was complete, she found lasting peace. Her dwelling now is eternal.

There is a stretch of highway going up into the mountains of western North Carolina that has been under construction for many years. It is rugged terrain. The North Carolina Department of Transportation has the task of blasting through boulders and mangled tree roots to carve a smooth pathway into the high country. Vehicles have been caught in rockslides and temporary road closings. Signs flash through the night, Proceed with Caution, as the road winds and twists through the hills, guiding drivers through the maze. When travelers living at the top of the mountain see the welcomed sign, End of Construction, they know they are nearing home. I have known many parents who live in that part of the state and who pace the floor knowing their teenagers are up and down that mountain all the time. Reaching their destinations safely brings relief.

Life can be like traveling a treacherous road. There are potholes that jolt us, detours that get us off course, and signs warning us of danger ahead. The destination of the soul and spirit is of utmost importance to God, so He offers us daily guidance. Some pay close attention to God's directions; others ignore them and speed past the flashing lights. But everyone eventually arrives at the final destination: death's door. This is where the soul is separated from the body.

Even on the cross, Jesus taught that death was a passage for the spirit into the presence of God (Luke 23:46). The psalmist declared, "God will redeem my soul from the power of the grave" (Psalm 49:15 NKJV). Have you committed your soul into the hands of its Maker? Are you following the caution signs that God has posted throughout His Guidebook, the Bible? "The highway of the upright is to depart from evil; He who keeps his way preserves his soul" (Proverbs 16:17 NKJV).

You may find yourself saying, "But, Billy, I'm nearing the end of life. I haven't been a bad person." There are many, young and old, who have said this as they have contemplated death, but it is my duty to speak the truth from God's Word: "For all have sinned and fall short of the glory of God" (Romans 3:23 NKJV).

During a visit to the Billy Graham Library, a woman relayed a story: "My sweet mother, seventy-six years old, who never did any wrong in my eyes, struggled with my belief that all people were born sinners, according to Scripture. I prayed for years that she would come to recognize her own sin and repent so that she would know the salvation of Christ alone and have the promise of eternity with Him. When I received a call that my mother was on her deathbed, I traveled from Europe to her home in Florida. She took my hand and said, 'My dear, when I'm gone, take heart. The Lord has saved me.' 'Mother, how did this come about?' 'When I could no longer do for myself and was committed to this bed of infirmity, I realized I had come to the end of myself; I had no more control over my life. I felt lost in my own house. The home health care attendant who has been coming would patiently read to me, sometimes from the Bible: "There is none righteous, no, not one" [Romans 3:10 NKJV]; "Now set your heart and your soul to seek the LORD your God" [1 Chronicles 22:19 NKJV]; and "for the Son of Man has come to seek and to save that which was lost" [Luke 19:10 NKJV].' That moment, for me, will never fade. When I met the dear lady who had faithfully led my mother to the Lord, I was stunned at her vitality of life. She was the same age as my mother. It gave me great comfort to know that God will use us—no matter our age—to minister to others if we make ourselves available."

The Bible says that "a true witness delivers souls" (Proverbs 14:25 NKJV). The living never run out of opportunity; the question is, do we take advantage of the opportunities that come to us as this home health care worker did? Sometimes death comes suddenly and unexpectedly. "I didn't even have a chance to say good-bye" is a lament I must have heard dozens of times. Even more tragic is the knowledge that you missed that last chance to share the Gospel.

As people grow older, the less surprised we are by their deaths, which often come only after an extended period of declining health. There even may be time for family members to gather and be with the dying person in the final hours. That is the way it was with Ruth. "Her body is beginning to shut down," her doctor told me frankly. "Her death may still be some days away, but the process has begun, and you need to be prepared." Two weeks later we gathered around her bedside as her breathing grew more shallow. I was seated by Ruth's bedside holding her hand, and our daughter Anne was standing beside me. Suddenly Anne said, "She is in Heaven."

Her breathing had stopped, and her hand slipped from mine. Her years of suffering were over; Ruth had entered her final home.

Memories of those final months will remain with me the rest of my life: her growing frailty, her suffering, her expressions of love, our times of prayer, her certainty—and even joy—that soon she would be in the presence of the Lord she had loved and served for so many years. As I think back over those days, the familiar words of Psalm 23 come to me with new meaning, for they exemplify Ruth's confidence as she sensed her time on earth was drawing to a close: "Yea, though I walk through the valley of the shadow of death, I will fear no evil: for thou art with me; thy rod and thy staff they comfort me. . . . Surely goodness and mercy shall follow me all the days of my life: and I will dwell in the house of the LORD for ever" (vv. 4, 6 KJV).

## LIVING WITH GRIEF

As I write this it has been four years since Ruth went home to be with the Lord. I feel her loss more keenly now. Not a day passes that I don't imagine her walking through my study door or us sitting together on our porch as we did so often, holding hands as the sun set over the mountaintops.

I have asked myself why this is the case; after all, shouldn't our grieving over the loss of a loved one fade as time passes? Yes, it should—and in some ways it has for me. But in other ways it hasn't, nor do I expect it to. One reason, I think, is because my strongest memory at the time of her death was of her last days—her weakness, her pain, her yearning for Heaven. Much as

I longed to have her stay with us, I also knew that for her, death would be a welcome release from the burdens of this life. But with the passing of time, memories of the happiness we shared over more than sixty-three years of marriage come to mind. I remember our last years together as my travels lessened and we had more time just to be together. Those were some of the best years of our lives—almost as if we were falling in love again. And with those memories has come a deeper sense of loss.

The other reason I still feel her death so deeply, I think, is because mingled with my grief is a new sense of expectancy—the certain knowledge that someday soon the Lord will come for me also, and before long Ruth and I will be reunited in Heaven. More than ever, I look forward to that day!

## GRIEVING OUR LOSSES

Grief is a reality; those who say that we shouldn't grieve the loss of loved ones "because they're better off now" have never understood the enormous hole that is left in our hearts when loved ones die. Yes, they may be better off if they are in Heaven—but we aren't better off. A major part of our lives has been ripped from us, and just as it takes time to heal from a major surgery, so it takes time to heal from the loss of loved ones. Paul's words to the believers in Thessalonica are true: "We do not . . . grieve like the rest of men, who have no hope" (1 Thessalonians 4:13). But we still grieve, and that is as it should be. Jesus wept as He stood by the tomb of His friend Lazarus even though He knew that shortly He would bring Lazarus back to life (John 11:35).

My experience may not be the same as yours may be, but grief comes eventually to us all. You may not have been touched as yet by the death of your spouse; you may not even have experienced the death of anyone close to you, such as a parent or grandparent. On the other hand, grief may have come into your life in cruel and tragic ways—the death of a child or of a relative or spouse suddenly taken from you by a heart attack or accident. But no matter what our present experience is, the Bible's words are true:

> There is a time for everything,
> and a season for every activity under heaven:
> a time to be born and a time to die. (Ecclesiastes 3:1–2)

## DEALING WITH OUR GRIEF

How should we cope with grief? Let me mention four steps that have helped me, not just as I have grieved Ruth's death but as I have dealt with the deaths of my parents; my brother (and best friend), Melvin; my sister Catherine; Ruth's mother and father; and other relatives and friends over the years.

### Accepting Your Feelings

First, don't be surprised by your grief or deny it or feel guilty over it. Even when the death of someone we love is expected, we still will miss him or her, and we still will grieve our loss. Don't be surprised, either, if it creeps up on you at unexpected times and takes you by surprise. "I thought I was over my grief after my husband died last year," a woman wrote me once, "but a few days ago someone walked by who reminded me of him, and suddenly the tears began to flow."

Grieving is a process, and it doesn't go away overnight—even when we know our loved ones' suffering has ended and they are now safely in Heaven. When death comes to someone we love, we may feel numb at first (particularly if the death is unexpected); people may even comment on how well we are handling our grief. But then the numbness wears off, and the reality of what has happened may send us into periods of great sadness and unrelenting sorrow. People who have never experienced grief often can't understand this, but that should not make us think we are abnormal nor should we deny our feelings and pretend everything is fine. "I told people I didn't understand why my friend didn't snap out of it and stop dwelling on her mother's death so much," one woman reportedly said. "But then my brother died, and now I understand."

## Looking to the Future

A second step I have found helpful in times of grief is this: don't focus only on the past, but also turn your heart and mind to the future. When someone close to us dies, we naturally focus on what that person meant to us in the past. We remember the good times we had, and how our love bound us together even in hard times. We sense, too, the crushing finality of death and realize as never before that the past is gone forever, and it will never be repeated. It's not wrong to do this; in fact, it is perfectly natural. Ruth often said when news came of the deaths of friends or relatives, "I'm happy for them, but sad for us."

But as time passes we also need to turn our thoughts to our own futures. That isn't easy to do; we don't want to face the pain and emptiness we know we are going to feel in the months and years ahead. It's easier to focus on the memories of the past. But we still have people who love us and need us, and we still have responsibilities. Most of all, God is not finished with us; He still has a plan for the remainder of our lives. Paul's words concerning his own spiritual journey apply to us even when we grieve: "One thing I do: Forgetting what is behind and straining toward what is ahead, I press on toward the goal to win the prize for which God has called me heavenward in Christ Jesus" (Philippians 3:13–14).

Sometimes, however, the future intrudes on us in ways we would rather avoid. No one wants to face the legal and financial issues that may need to be settled shortly after someone's death; no one wants to face the task of cleaning out a spouse's closet or desk. I am grateful that my children were willing to help me with these practical matters after Ruth's death. At the same time, don't be forced into making hasty or ill-conceived decisions that you will later regret.

Forcing our hearts and minds to look toward the future means accepting what has happened and—little by little—learning to live with it. It means also that we begin resuming our normal activities and contacts—not necessarily all at once, but nevertheless resisting the temptation to remain withdrawn. It may take a deliberate act of the will on our part to restart our normal routines, but it is important to do so. "No one understands what I'm going through" is a common feeling among those who have lost someone close to them. Even if it is true, however, don't let it become an excuse for remaining isolated or inactive.

## Helping Others

A third step in finding healing for grief is this: in time, begin reaching out to others who need your help. I heard once about a pastor who always ended his sermons with these words: "Remember: everyone you are going to meet this week is carrying a heavy burden." Over the years I have found this to be true; I have never met a person who wasn't weighed down by some kind of problem or burden. But God wants to help carry everyone's burdens—one way He does that is by sending someone into the person's life who can share the burden. Grief is a heavy burden, and we need to be willing to have others reach out and help us carry it instead of trying to shoulder it alone.

Paul reminds us, "Carry each other's burdens, and in this way you will fulfill the law of Christ" (Galatians 6:2); and "Rejoice with those who rejoice; mourn with those who mourn" (Romans 12:15). All around you are others who have burdens, and God can use your experience to encourage and help them. Are there those in your church or neighborhood carrying a burden of grief right now? Ask God to help you be a friend to them. More than most people, you can understand what they are going through, and you can help relieve the weight of their burden by your concern. Sometimes all they need is someone who will listen. Remember that God is "the Father of compassion and the God of all comfort, who comforts us in all our troubles, so that we can comfort those in any trouble with the comfort we ourselves have received from

God" (2 Corinthians 1:3–4). And when we reach out to others, we help not only them but also ourselves because we are distracted from our own grief.

### Turning to God

The final step in dealing with our grief is also the most important. Take your burden of grief to God. God knows what you are going through, and He loves you and wants to help you. Remember that He knows what it is to grieve because He had to watch as His only Son was put to death. Jesus was "a man of sorrows, and acquainted with grief" (Isaiah 53:3 KJV). But Jesus said, "Blessed are those who mourn, for they will be comforted" (Matthew 5:4).

How does God help us cope with grief? First, He assures us of His presence. We are never alone if we know Christ; He lives within us by His Spirit. Even when you don't feel His presence, it doesn't change the fact that He is with you every moment of the day. God's promise is for you:

> So do not fear, for I am with you;
>     do not be dismayed, for I am your God.
> I will strengthen you and help you;
>     I will uphold you with my righteous right hand.
>     (Isaiah 41:10)

He also assures us of His promises. God cannot lie—and from one end of the Bible to the other, He has given us "his very great and precious promises" (2 Peter 1:4). Read them, learn them, memorize them, trust them, and let them grow and bear fruit in your soul.

Shortly after Ruth's death I leafed through one of her old Bibles. She had underlined hundreds of verses, often adding a brief comment of her own in the margin. She especially had underlined passages in the Psalms that spoke of God's promise to be with us in times of hardship or sorrow or loneliness. In the midst of your grief, turn daily to God's Word, and let its promises encourage and sustain you. Remember to:

> Cast your cares on the LORD
> and he will sustain you;
> he will never let the righteous fall. (Psalm 55:22)

Then God also helps us by assuring us of His goodness. When we lose a loved one, usually all we can think about is our own grief and how empty our lives are going to be. We even may be angry at God for taking our loved one from us. Instead we should remember God's blessings and have a spirit of gratitude—gratitude for the life of our loved one, gratitude for all he or she meant to us, gratitude for the years God gave us together, and most of all gratitude that death ushers a saved soul into God's presence forever. A daily "attitude of gratitude" will do much to move us beyond our sorrow.

## REMEMBERING YOUR FRIENDS

You may not be dealing with the death of a loved one right now; you may even feel it's a bit morbid to give much thought to it, at least until it happens. But even if you won't be touched by grief yourself for some time to come, others around you will be—friends, coworkers, relatives, even casual acquaintances. How can you help them deal with their grief, even if it doesn't touch you personally?

It is not always easy to help someone who is grieving; some people are proud or intensely private, and they may resent our efforts to help them. In general, however, I have found at least three ways we often can help people who are grieving.

### Tell Them You Care

"I never realized how much a simple note or a sympathy card could mean until my father died," a man said to me once, "but they meant more to me than I'd ever imagined. They let me know that people cared, and that was very encouraging."

Caring can take many forms—from helping them make funeral arrangements to simply telling them how much their loved one meant to you. It may mean listening to them as they recount the events of the last few days or weeks. Over the years Ruth must have dispensed hundreds of gallons of homemade soup to families in our community who had gathered for a loved one's funeral. Look for some way you can help, and then do it even if it is just washing the dishes or keeping a register of visitors. But be sensitive; some people are reluctant to accept help from people who are not close friends.

### Keep in Touch

Often when someone dies, there is a flurry of activity at first—relatives gather, people call, flowers arrive, and people come by to express sympathy. But time passes, and so does our concern. "At first everyone called or stopped by," one woman wrote me, "but it's been six months since Jim died, and now no one calls to see how I'm doing. It's as if I've been forgotten."

But it shouldn't be this way—especially among Christians. The Bible says, "Show mercy and compassion to one another" (Zechariah 7:9). One former accountant devotes his retirement years to helping those who have recently lost a spouse deal with insurance or legal papers they may not understand. I heard about another man who spends several days a week driving older people who recently lost a spouse to doctors' appointments.

### Pray for Them

Pray that they will experience God's comfort, and pray, too, that they will turn to Christ for the peace and hope they need. If you had lost a loved one recently, wouldn't you be glad to learn that others were praying for you?

## NEARING HOME WITH GOD'S COMFORT

Death is always an intruder even when it is expected. It disrupts our lives and brings grief in its wake. No one welcomes death's legacy of pain and emptiness and loneliness—but God has not abandoned us, and even in the midst of life's greatest sorrows His Word is still true: "Never will I leave you; never will I forsake you" (Hebrews 13:5). This is a wonderful promise, filled with assurance, in the face of sorrow and death. Through God's Word we are able to draw from His presence that lives within us through

His Holy Spirit. The Lord also sends comfort through others, and we need to ask Him to reveal those around us who are praying for God's comfort because He often sends it through His servants.

It always warms my heart to read Paul's salutations and greetings in his epistles to those who have served him and with him in ministry. A particular reference is especially insightful: "Greet Rufus, chosen in the Lord, and his mother, who has been a mother to me, too" (Romans 16:13). Rufus happened to be the son of Simon the Cyrene, who was called out from the crowd to carry the cross for Jesus.

Scripture does not mention Paul's parents, but in this passage our hearts are touched by the apostle's loving acknowledgment of this dear mother. She is the wife of Simon, and while we are not given details, it is apparent that this elderly mother cared for Paul during his ministry.

Can you imagine the conversations that Paul and Rufus must have had with Simon's wife as she recounted the day her husband was called upon to help carry the cross of Jesus up Calvary's road to His destination of death? Paul surely recounted his trip on the road to Damascus. His destination that day was to capture Christians and return them to Jerusalem where they also would face death. Can you fathom the joy this mother felt to know that her son, Rufus, was serving with the man whom the Lord miraculously saved and called to bring the saving Gospel to the world? She obviously grew to love Paul as one of her own and made a significant impression on Paul as Scripture records. What a blessing this elderly mother would have missed had she not opened her home and heart to the beloved apostle Paul.

While many older folks are not able to care for themselves, many are still capable and can care for others in various ways. We often find that our own loads are not as heavy when we begin helping others. Our choices determine our destiny. When we make choices with the Lord Jesus at the center, life's journey can be purposeful and filled with hope that one day we will be reunited with all those who have impacted our lives.

# 7 INFLUENCING THE IMPRESSIONABLE

I have been reminded of your sincere faith, which
first lived in your grandmother . . . and in your
mother . . . and, I am persuaded, now lives in you also.

—2 TIMOTHY 1:5

Wise counsel to the younger is the duty of the aged.

—UNKNOWN

A new generation of caregivers takes control of kids," read a *Washington Post* headline in 2010. The article, based on a 2007 Pew Research Center study, reported that one in ten children in the United States now lives with a grandparent. In today's world with all the controversy over Medicare, senior citizens, social security, and struggling to find caregivers for the aged, this is a breathtaking reversal in roles. Multiple reasons are cited for this remarkable statistic: parents losing their jobs and having to leave home to find work, parents on active military duty, parents incarcerated, orphaned children, court injunctions against drug-addicted parents, single parents battling life-threatening diseases, teen pregnancy, and the list goes on. A subhead in the article shouted, "Grandparents to the rescue!"

The stories are startling: One grandmother reported finding her two-month-old grandson on her doorstep when she responded to a knock at the door at 3:00 a.m. He had been left there by her drug-addicted daughter. A grandfather was asked if he resented his retirement being interrupted by having to raise his young grandchildren due to their parents' deaths in an automobile accident. He said, "It is my duty. I certainly don't want strangers raising my son's children. Besides, what are grandparents for?" Some grandparents resent the intrusion; others see it as a blessing and are grateful for the opportunity to provide stability in the midst of emotional trauma difficult for any youth to cope with. For some grandparents, there is a tremendous financial hardship that accompanies their new role. Many live on meager incomes and cannot return to work for myriad reasons.[1]

One hundred years ago, similar conditions would not have presented the same challenges. Multigenerational homes were common, particularly in farm communities that were the backbone of our nation. Society did not look down on homesteads where the grandparents lived with a married child and spouse and their several children. They all sat around the dinner table daily having collectively worked the farm, maintained household chores, and prepared the meals. Everyone pitched in. Then they would all retreat to the front porch in the cool of the evening or gather around the fireplace to keep warm in the winter. They would laugh, share stories, and plan to do it all again the next day. Children saw their parents respecting their grandparents, an example that taught honor toward the elderly. The grandparents were grateful both for the hustle and bustle of youth and for the opportunity to support and guide their adult children in parenting. Many from the older generation often said that it increased their vitality and zest for life. While not every family situation was that picturesque, multi-generational homes weren't a bad concept. Strong family ties grew strong, reliable character, and I believe young people who know nothing of that era have missed out on important lessons.

My point is that grandparents and great-grandparents today often dismiss the importance of their family role. Respect must be earned and given. While society has belittled the impact of the older generations, the elderly have too easily relinquished their roles without much thought. The Bible tells us to care for our family members, especially our immediate families (1 Timothy 5:8). The example must start with those who have lived the longest. Some may say that the elderly are no longer relevant in society, but that doesn't mean we should take a backseat. When the family is destroyed, society eventually disintegrates. Our nation is experiencing this today. A dear friend said one day, "It's time we let the young people lead. We had our day. We did it our way. Now it's their turn."

I am grateful that my children were influenced by their grandparents. My father died when my children were quite young, and my mother lived two hours away, but the children often visited her until her death in 1981. The children, however, grew up in walking distance of Ruth's parents. They spent much time with my children and made a profound impact in the lives of each. Dr. Bell entertained them with his stories about time spent in China as a missionary doctor. When he got to the gory details, Ruth's mother would scold him for saying such things. The children would laugh with delight, coaxing their grandfather to continue. They still talk about it today. They also refer often to the strength they still draw from their grandparents' experiences and wisdom. After all, it is part of their heritage, and they have passed it on to their children and grandchildren. This is a lasting legacy.

I realize that this is not everyone's story. There are many who have never known the love of home and family. Many have dark stories of abuse and an overwhelming lack of love and acceptance. Society seems to lose more ground with each passing generation. An elderly couple admitted they had "no earthly idea" how to influence their teenage grandchildren—they simply could not relate to them. In response, I believe that is, perhaps, the problem—we are looking for an *earthly* solution. We should, instead, try looking into God's Word. That's where we will find the answers.

Peer pressure is a very real thing that impacts individuals and their influence. The Bible says,

> If you speak good words rather than worthless ones,
>> you will be my spokesman.
> You must influence them;
>> do not let them influence you! (Jeremiah 15:19 NLT)

In my day boys felt the peer pressure to smoke. My children's generation felt strong pressure to experiment with drugs. My grand-children's generation has been assaulted with promiscuous sex at nearly every age and level of society. Because the Word of God has been absent from our public school system for decades, and because families have virtually stopped attending church together, there are only shades of godly influence that instruct them to live moral lives and reverence God.

It is striking to read how the young are influencing the elderly. One rather young grandmother made excuses for living with a man. She said, "My granddaughter thinks I'm very cool." This is a far cry from life on the farm when a granddaughter would gain insight from a loving grandmother's instruction to "teach what is good" (Titus 2:3). The older generation should be looking for ways to encourage the younger because they are constantly bom-barded with wrong teaching, poor examples, and pressure tactics.

A reporter interviewing a 104-year-old woman asked, "What is the best thing about being 104?" She simply replied, "No peer pressure." This may bring a smile because there is so much truth in it. As the old grow older, we are more likely to forget what it was to be young and impressionable.

George Beverly Shea enjoys life at 102. He considers me his younger friend. Those who are blessed with living a healthy and full life for a century and counting are in a class all their own. Many often ask why Bev can so effectively connect with the young. I believe the reason is that Bev embraces his age with grace and humor and people are drawn to that authenticity. They are invigorated by his good spirit and his testimony to what the

Lord Jesus means to him. He doesn't try to redress his beliefs in order to be accepted by those younger than him. And I find it interesting how many young people visit him and ask him to play the organ. We, the older generation, often sell young people short by giving them what we think they want instead of sharing our experiences. To us, our experiences are old news. To the young, it is information they have never heard and considered. Stanford University held a forum a decade ago on aging and invited young people to participate in the discussion. The question: "Why is aging a young person's issue?"[2] One student reportedly responded, "Because we're all on the same journey, and I'd like to know what others learned along the way."

What a privilege we have to prepare the way for those who are watching. Do we really take this to heart? We are allowing Satan to snuff out our influence by making us think that no one really cares. In writing this book, I was given comments that were found on a blog from young people discussing the difference between the young and old generations. It stated, "We need both generations in society for what they contribute. The younger one questions, challenges, and sparks change; the older one puts on the brakes sometimes, providing the wisdom of experience [that can help us make wise decisions for our lives]."[3]

While this may not represent all younger generations, it does reveal that not all of them resist hearing from their elders. The question we are faced with is, are we shunning the opportunities that come our way to be an influence for good, or are we being irresponsible in our encounters with those who may take to heart what we have to contribute? The Bible instructs generations to pass on what has been learned. Our youth need to say with the psalmist,

> We have heard with our ears, O God,
>      Our fathers have told us,
>      The deeds You did in their days,
>      In days of old. (Psalm 44:1 NKJV)

Long after you are gone, what will your children and grandchildren remember about you? Sometimes the elderly miss their opportunities. They are too engrossed in their ailments and can be solely responsible for running people off—even grandchildren.

Some time ago a young man wrote to me and said, "I wish I could say I have good memories of my grandmother, but all I remember about her is that she seemed very old, and she was always grumbling and complaining about everything." Another wrote, "My grandfather always made our visits fun, but after we left we would never hear from him." A disheartened daughter stated, "My parents are so wrapped up in themselves that all they've been interested in since they retired is having a good time. I wonder if I'll be like that when I get older. I hope not."

I hope not, too, because this is not the way God wants us to spend our latter years. Complaining, being unengaged or self-indulgent—what kind of impression are these attitudes sure to make on those who follow us? What will they remember about us if we are like this? More important, what do these attitudes teach them about life and how it ought to be lived? The answer is: very little, and nothing that is good.

But God doesn't want us to waste our latter years or spend them in superficial, meaningless pursuits. Instead He wants us to use them in whatever ways we can to influence those who will come after us. God wants us to finish well—and one of the ways we do this is by passing on our values and our faith to those who will follow us.

## LEAVING A LEGACY

Our children are not like computers; we can't program them so they will always do exactly what we want them to do or turn out exactly the way we wish they would. It is one of life's mysteries: two children can be brought up in the same family and in the same way yet turn out to be exact opposites as they grow older. Parents know every child is different, and even with the best training, some children may reject our efforts to guide them. The best we can do is provide the right environment—love them and train them and pray for them and provide them the tools they will need to make wise decisions as they grow older. We do this both by our teaching and by our example—in other words, both by what we say and by what we do.

As parents we have a direct influence on our children; later on our influence on our grandchildren probably will be much less direct. Sometimes this isn't the case, of course; due to death or divorce or some other situation, grandparents may have to step in and assume the role of parents. But by and large our opportunities to influence both our own children and our grandchildren fade as we grow older.

But that does not mean we don't have any influence on them—because we do. Nor does it mean our influence is insignificant—because it isn't. In fact, it may turn out to be one of the most important things we will ever do. Even if we don't have grandchildren or if we are childless or single, we still have an important and unique legacy to pass on to the next generation—and beyond. They are observing us, and they will learn from our lives.

Think about it a moment: How will they learn about the realities of old age and how to cope with them? Or how will they learn about the importance of building their lives on a strong foundation of faith in Christ and His Word? Or how will they discover the difference that Christ can make in someone's life, especially as they grow older? The answer is obvious: they will learn these things by observing those who are already older.

## Our Greatest Legacy

The greatest legacy you can pass on to your children and grandchildren is not your money or the other material things you have accumulated in life. The greatest legacy you can pass on to them is the legacy of your character and your faith. The same is true for other young people who know us and observe us even if they aren't related to us.

This, after all, is what our grandchildren and others who knew us will remember about us after we are gone—for better or for worse. If our character is bad, marked by greed or thoughtlessness or anger or bitterness or selfishness or irresponsibility or a lack of integrity or any other negative quality, this is how we will be remembered. But if our character and integrity have been shaped by Christ over the years, they can't help but see this and remember it.

Why is faith our greatest legacy? Because the memory of what we were like—not just our personalities but our character and our faith—has the potential to influence others for Christ.

My parents had a profound impact on me. My mother's kind and gentle character and concern for the spiritual welfare of others are reaping fruit still today. Although her formal education was limited, she loved the Bible and spent a great deal of time teaching the Bible to others. I recall also with deep gratitude my father's example of honesty, integrity, discipline, and hard work.

I remember as a young man observing an older couple who lived in our community. They enjoyed one another's company, never realizing the impact they were making on those watching from afar. Over the years countless others have influenced me and changed me by the examples of their lives—although I am sure they were unaware of it. The same has probably been true of people in your life. Our greatest impact on others often comes not from what we say but from what we do.

## Our Greatest Hope

What is your greatest hope for your children and grandchildren (and for others outside your family who are part of the next generation)? Is it that they will become men and women of compassion, honesty, morality, responsibility, selflessness, loyalty, discipline, and sacrifice? Your hope should be that they will become men and women of faith, trusting Jesus Christ as their Savior and seeking to follow Him as the Master of their lives every day.

While we cannot make this decision for others, we can show them the way by being an example of Christ's love and of His power to transform every life that is submitted to Him.

A word of caution, however, is in order here. We cannot pretend to be something we are not; a Christlike character cannot be faked. If Christ is not real to us or if we haven't learned to walk with Him and submit our lives to Him every day, then our spiritual impact on those who follow us will be far less than it might have been. Young people are very sensitive to hypocrisy; if they sense it in us, they will dismiss our pretenses and pay no attention to our advice. On the other hand, if they can sense our faith is sincere and our love is authentic, then they will respect us and take us seriously (even when they know we are not perfect).

This is why it is important to begin building our lives on the solid foundation of Jesus Christ now, instead of waiting until it is too late and the problems of old age overwhelm us. Every gardener knows that mature fruit does not appear overnight. It takes time to grow—and so does the fruit of the Spirit in our lives. The Bible urges us to "be mature and complete, not lacking anything" (James 1:4).

## BRIDGING THE GAP

In practical terms how can we impact those who may be separated from us by as much as four or five decades, or thousands of miles? Over the years Ruth and I tried to follow several practices in our relationships with our grandchildren (and now great-grandchildren—forty-three in number, as I write this)—although I know we weren't perfect. Perhaps they will be helpful to you.

## Pray Consistently

Pray consistently for your family. God knows their needs far better than you do, and He "is able to do immeasurably more than all we ask or imagine" (Ephesians 3:20). God is able to do what we cannot do, especially within our families. We have all heard the old expression, "Out of sight, out of mind." Don't let that be true of your family; pray for them regularly.

Don't pray only in general terms (the kind of prayer that vaguely asks God to bless them). Make your prayers specific, and make them daily. Pray not only that God will keep them safe but that He will guard them from the temptations and evils that assail young people today. Pray that God will give them a desire to do what is right and avoid what is wrong, and to seek His will for their lives as they grow older. Pray about any decisions you know they will be making or difficulties you know they are facing. Let them know you are praying for them, not because you are trying to intrude in their lives but because you love them and care deeply about what happens to them. Most of all, pray that they will open their hearts and lives to Jesus Christ and become His followers.

## Keep in Touch

Sometimes consistent communication isn't easy; families become scattered, and we also have to avoid giving the impression that we are trying to interfere in their private lives. But take advantage of whatever opportunities you do have. In some families this may come daily; in others, it is limited to the occasional phone call or birthday greeting. I know grandparents who have gone out of their way to learn how to e-mail or to register on one of the new social media sites because it gives them an opportunity to stay in touch with their grandchildren.

It is important as well to let them know you love them and care deeply about what happens to them. Not long ago as I was waiting for a doctor's appointment, a woman casually asked me if I had any grandchildren. When I told her I had nineteen, she gasped in horror. "Nineteen!" she exclaimed. "How do you stand it? I only have two, and they drive me crazy. I can't imagine having to put up with nineteen!" Her reaction amused me at first, but it also saddened me. Your grandchildren may not dress the way you wish they would or listen to your kind of music, but God gave them to you, and He loves them. They are one of God's gifts to you, so let them know you love them, both by your words and by your actions.

## Encourage Them

The Bible says, "Encourage one another and build each other up" (1 Thessalonians 5:11). After Saul of Tarsus (later called Paul) met Christ on the road to Damascus, one man befriended him and helped him, and he later became Saul's companion on his first missionary journey. That man was Barnabas, "which means Son of Encouragement" (Acts 4:36).

It is tempting to lecture our grandchildren or tell them what we think they are doing wrong, and there may be a place for that occasionally. But don't major in the negatives! They need to know we love them, and most of all that God loves them. Encourage them when they deserve it, and when they don't, encourage them to think about taking a different path. Learn, too, to "forgive and forget" if they are thoughtless or do something that hurts us.

At the same time, avoid the pitfalls. For example, it is easy to show favoritism, even in our families. We may relate to one grandchild more than another and unconsciously spend more time with that one or give him or her more gifts. But the Bible says, "Do nothing out of favoritism" (1 Timothy 5:21). God made each of them, and He loves each of them—and so should we. Our loving and fair treatment of each should build up their faith in themselves and in God.

## Remember Your Place

We are not our grandchildren's parents, and we have to be careful not to step over the line and create tension by interfering with their parents' work in their lives. We also need to avoid causing tension or conflict by taking sides in family disputes. Let the Bible's admonition be your guide: "Above all, love each other deeply, because love covers over a multitude of sins" (1 Peter 4:8).

## Be an Example

Remember, your children and grandchildren learn more about you through observing your actions and attitudes. Do they see Christ in you? Will they remember you as someone who was a living example of His compassion and love? Even when hard times come or the disabilities of old age overtake you, will they recall your underlying peace and joy in their midst? May they remember you as someone whose life was changed by Jesus Christ—just as theirs can be.

## FIXING BROKEN RELATIONSHIPS

How do we restore a legacy that has been marred by something that may have happened many years ago, but continues to haunt us because it was never resolved? Often these have to do with broken relationships that have never been healed. Perhaps this has been true in your own life. If so, face it honestly, and do whatever you can to change it. As we grow older and look back over our lives, how will we view these unresolved conflicts?

"My mother and I always had a difficult relationship," one woman wrote me recently, "and for the last ten years we didn't even speak. Now she's gone, and I'd give anything to have just one minute with her to tell her I'm sorry." Another woman wrote, "Twelve years ago I told my son I didn't want anything more to do with him. Now I'm wondering if I did the right thing. I feel so alone, and he's the only family I have." One man's letter included this comment: "I guess you could say I burned my bridges with my family over twenty years ago. They weren't perfect, but I have to admit I was the main problem. I'd like to get back in contact, but they've let me know they aren't interested."

Each of these (and hundreds more I could cite) tells a slightly different story, but the basic problem is the same: a broken relationship that has never been healed. Each also has another common theme: regret—regret over what happened, regret over the years that have been lost, regret because the time for healing has passed.

Don't come to the end of your life and look back with regret over a hurt that could have been forgiven or a relationship that could have been healed—if you had only seized the initiative and taken the first step. Why don't we do this? Often it is because of pride; we hate to admit we were wrong or at least that we had a part in causing the split. Sometimes it is because we are afraid of being rebuffed or of opening our lives to still more hurt. But whatever the reason, do not let it keep you from seeking to heal the hurts and conflicts of the past.

It is not always possible to mend a broken relationship, of course; some people simply refuse to be reconciled with someone who has hurt them or whom they have hurt. Some people also refuse to accept responsibility for what they have done, always blaming someone else for what happened. If so, you probably can't solve their problems—but you can solve yours by being willing to go the extra mile to try to be reconciled with someone who has turned against you. You should "make every effort to live in peace with all men and to be holy" (Hebrews 12:14), and "if it is possible, as far as it depends on you, live at peace with everyone" (Romans 12:18). Peace isn't possible in every case, but we are to make the effort.

Ask God to make a forgiving spirit part of your legacy, not only reconciling you with others but also passing on an example of Christ's forgiveness and grace to those who come after you. It isn't easy; it will take much thought, wisdom, and prayer. But it will be one of the most important things you ever do.

## NEARING HOME WITH A LASTING LEGACY

*Forgiveness* is one of the most beautiful words in the human vocabulary and is best illustrated by God's forgiveness of sin. When

God's people practice forgiveness with their fellow man, sweetness replaces harshness. A marvelous example of this is revealed in the life of Joseph, when he forgave his brothers for selling him into slavery as a young man. Joseph assured his brothers that while they intended to do evil to their younger brother, God meant it for good by using him to save many people during the famine that swept the land (Genesis 50:20). Because of Joseph's demonstration of forgiveness, he was greatly blessed of God in his old age. The Bible says, "Joseph saw Ephraim's children to the third generation. The children of Machir, the son of Manasseh, were also brought up on Joseph's knees" (Genesis 50:23 NKJV). What a legacy! The grandchildren and great-grandchildren of this hero of faith enjoyed fellowship with their grandfather, Joseph. If we cannot find it in our hearts to forgive within our own family, how can we practice this attribute of Christ with others and know God's blessings?

The Bible says that great blessing comes when we see our children's children (Psalm 128:6). Do we fully comprehend the blessings that come from the hand of God? May we take advantage of the opportunities to influence our families for Christ.

# 8 A FOUNDATION THAT LASTS

Each one should be careful how he builds. For no one can lay any foundation other than the one already laid, which is Jesus Christ.

—1 CORINTHIANS 3:10–11

God buries His workmen but carries on His work.

—CHARLES WESLEY

Young people never see themselves as growing old. They are caught up in the age of youthfulness, bursting with excitement that energizes their hopes and dreams. I can recall those days. In the late thirties, I was a nineteen-year-old student at Florida Bible Institute (now Trinity College) located on the outskirts of Tampa. I, along with some other students, met an aged evangelist by the name of Judson W. Van DeVenter. He had ministered with J. Wilbur Chapman (who had traveled and preached with D. L. Moody and later became a mentor to Billy Sunday). Mr. Van DeVenter taught hymnology at the school and wrote many notable songs such as "I Surrender All" and "Saved Through Jesus' Blood."

Mr. Van DeVenter had some orange groves in the Sunshine State, and when he could no longer work, the young fellows at the school went to pick the fruit before the frost fell. We found ourselves looking after the elderly preacher. I remember how appreciative he was when the younger guys would lend a helping hand. He benefited from our labor, and while we never imagined being that old and may not have understood at the time, we drew from his example. Such encounters contribute to life's foundation.

J. W. Van DeVenter died in Temple Terrace, Florida, in 1939 at age eighty-four. As an energetic Bible student, I could not imagine living that long and needing the level of care that he required. It seemed he could do little for himself. Now that I am ninety-two, my gratitude for Mr. Van DeVenter is deeper. Respect for others grows as we ourselves become dependent upon others. Looking back on providing for Mr. Van DeVenter gives me a greater appreciation for those who so lovingly care for me today. I can only hope in my senior state that I am building bridges for those following behind me as I encourage them on the roads they travel.

For those of us nearing home, our steps may indeed be slow, but they need not be without purpose. Younger generations follow us on our last mile of the way. What does that tell us? We are still leading. But are we leading victoriously? Are we paving the way for those who follow in our footsteps? Perhaps we should even ask ourselves, "Are our footsteps worth following?" The answer is yes if we are following the footsteps of the Lord Jesus Christ and our bridges are built on the solid rock of His foundation. He alone lifts our cares and lightens our burdens.

## SHIFTING FOUNDATION OR SURE FOUNDATION

No one escapes life without difficulties. Some experience bad health even in their youth. Some born into wealth lose everything. Some seek love and find only rejection time and again. Without a firm foundation, life's load is harder to bear. God has a purpose for each of us, and He desires that we build upon Him, the very foundation He has put in place. Scripture speaks of craftsmen fastening the work of their hands with pegs "that it might not totter" (Isaiah 41:7 NKJV). When Christ's hands were pierced by spikes and fastened to the cross, He became our secure foundation. D. L. Moody once said, "Give your life to Christ: He can do more with it than you can."

Recently I heard about a family who built a house several years ago in the Appalachian Mountains not far from our home. The site was on a hillside with a beautiful view overlooking the nearby valley and facing a range of mountains in the distance. After they drew their plans and chose their builder, the project proceeded on schedule, and some months later their new house was completed. They were delighted with the result and soon were settled into the home of their dreams.

But after a year or so, their dream turned into a nightmare. The first hint of trouble was a slight depression in the soil around a certain section of the foundation; then as time went on, the depression deepened and cracks began to appear in the walls of the house. They became alarmed and called in a structural engineer to investigate. He discovered that part of the concrete for the foundation had been poured over a pit filled with debris—old tree stumps, loose rocks, even wood left over from their construction project. As this wood decayed, the ground gave way, and the walls began to shift, making the whole house dangerously unstable. Whether by ignorance or neglect, the contractor had built their house on a defective foundation, and his error proved both costly and time-consuming to correct.

Just as this house needed a solid foundation, so we need a solid foundation for our lives—an unchanging system of beliefs, goals, and moral values that will keep us stable and secure, even in the midst of life's storms. No matter our age, nothing prepares us for the future like a solid moral and spiritual foundation based on God's will for our lives.

As I was reviewing this chapter, the world learned of a 9.0 earthquake and massive tsunami that devastated parts of northern Japan, causing thousands of deaths and even slightly shifting the earth's axis. I was grieved by the suffering and loss of those who survived, and my first reaction was to pray for them and ask God to help us assist them in whatever ways we could. My son Franklin immediately went to the affected area and began working with Japanese churches to bring aid to those whose lives had been turned upside down by the disaster.

I couldn't help but think of those who had once lived there and now had lost everything. They had built their houses on what they assumed were secure foundations; living in an earthquake-prone area, many probably had taken extra precautions. But when the ground suddenly shifted beneath their feet and the tsunami's massive wall of water rushed across their land, those foundations crumbled, leading to one of the greatest natural disasters in recent memory.

Terrible events like this remind us of what can happen if we build our lives on the wrong foundation—on one that may seem adequate in normal times but can't withstand life's stresses and strains. Tragically, however, many people never stop to think about this or examine the foundations on which they are building their lives. They assume they are on the right road and their foundations will always be secure. For some the foundation may be self-indulgence or pleasure or entertainment. Others build upon financial success or social position. Still others think that if they can only find the right person . . . or discover the ideal place to live . . . or clinch the best-paying job . . . then they will always be happy and secure.

But in their quiet moments they may wonder if it's really true. Perhaps a personal crisis—an unexpected illness, the rebellion of a child, a financial reversal—reveals the foundation for what it really is: unstable and insecure. Or perhaps they finally reach their goals and achieve all they have ever wanted—only to discover success has left them empty and restless and bored. They find themselves saying with the writer of Ecclesiastes,

> When I surveyed all that my hands had done
>    and what I had toiled to achieve,
> everything was meaningless, a chasing after the wind. (2:11)

Their hopes and dreams are shattered, leaving them confused and disillusioned and wondering what went wrong. Maybe this has happened to you.

When we build on shaky foundations, problems will come. This is certainly true when we replace Christ with other things: we put ourselves first—our dreams, our ambitions, our hopes, our goals, our appearance, our health, our possessions. We may even experience a measure of happiness and contentment for a time. "After all," we say to ourselves, "isn't this what life is all about? Isn't this the way we're supposed to live? Isn't this the way everyone else is living—or at least trying to live?" But sooner or later the shaky foundation is revealed for what it really is. Then troubles come (as they inevitably do), cracks appear, and the foundation starts to crumble. Sadly, we become like the man in Jesus' parable "who built his house on sand. The rain came down, the streams rose, and the winds blew and beat against that house, and it fell with a great crash" (Matthew 7:26–27).

Why is it that money, success, and pleasure bring no lasting satisfaction? Why don't they provide us with a solid foundation for successful living, especially as we grow older? Because they ignore one of life's greatest truths: we don't have just bodies and minds, but we also have souls, also called spirits. If we ignore this truth—if we feed our bodies but starve our souls—our lives will be incomplete and unfulfilled, and we will find ourselves weak and unprepared for life's inevitable challenges. Sooner or later the storms of life will overwhelm us, and we will discover that we have built our lives on foundations of sand.

Still it's easy to focus only on physical well-being or emotional happiness as we prepare for the future; we are bombarded with messages about them all the time. Financial advisors suggest that all we need to do to prepare for the future is to make the right investments. Health experts urge us to eat the right foods and take the right vitamins and get the right exercise so we will be healthy and happy and well liked. Publishers and TV infomercials promote a steady stream of products offering the latest advice on gaining success or overcoming life's problems or keeping old age at bay. Even cosmetics companies get into the act, claiming their products will turn back the clock and make us look younger. I read recently that Americans spend almost sixty billion dollars a year on antiaging products—a sum that is expected to increase 10 percent a year into the foreseeable future.

It is not necessarily wrong to be concerned about some of these things, of course. We should save for the future, and we should take care of our physical bodies and emotional health. But is this all it takes to prepare for the future?

The answer is no; even the securest financial plan and the finest health care aren't enough to hold us steady when the challenges come. Will a full bank account satisfy you when disability takes away your freedom or death robs you of someone you love? Will robust health shield you against the storms of loneliness or grief or financial insecurity that often besiege us as the aging process advances? Jesus said, "Is not life more important than food, and the body more important than clothes?" (Matthew 6:25). We need something more, something deeper and unshakable, something that will see us through life's hard times. We need a solid foundation beneath our lives—a foundation that will give us strength and stability no matter what happens. And the time to build it is now.

God does not want us to drift aimlessly through life, desperately seeking happiness and security and peace—but never finding them. Nor does He want us to build our lives on an unstable or impermanent foundation. God has already provided the foundation we need!

When Ruth and I were planning to build our home many years ago, a friend of ours offered to have an engineer he knew evaluate our building site, which we gladly welcomed. His tests revealed that under certain conditions the soil where we were planning to build might shift after a period of prolonged rain. At his recommendation the builder dug down through the surface soil to the bedrock and poured concrete pilings to make our house stable and secure. It proved to be the right solution.

We need a foundation that is as solid as that bedrock. Only God can provide it. Jesus Christ is the bedrock on which we need to build our lives. As we commit our lives to Him and grow in our relationship with Him, we discover He truly is the solid foundation we need. Every other foundation proves false. The Bible says, "Together, we are his house, built on the foundation of the apostles and prophets. And the cornerstone is Christ Jesus himself" (Ephesians 2:20 NLT).

## CHRIST, THE SURE FOUNDATION

Why should we build our lives on Christ? The first reason is because of who He is. Jesus Christ wasn't just a great religious teacher who walked on earth some two thousand years ago. The Bible says He was far more than that: He was God in human flesh. This is what we celebrate every Christmas—and this is what we should celebrate every day of our lives. The Bible tells us that on that first Christmas, God did something you and I can barely imagine: He came down from Heaven and became a man. That man was Jesus, who was both fully divine and fully human.

Do you want to know what God is like? Look at Jesus, for He was God in human flesh. The Bible says, "He is the image of the invisible God. . . . For in Christ all the fullness of the Deity lives in bodily form" (Colossians 1:15; 2:9). The proof was His resurrection from the dead, which confirmed not only His victory over sin and death and Satan and Hell but also the truth of His divine nature. His teachings aren't just the musings of a profound philosopher or religious teacher; they are God's message to us. His deeds of mercy weren't just the actions of a particularly compassionate individual; they were a demonstration of God's love and concern for each one of us.

Second, Christ should be our foundation because of what He did for us. Our greatest need is to be reconciled to God and become part of His family—but one insurmountable barrier stands in the way, and that is our sin. Sin separates us from God and brings us under His judgment, and no matter how hard we try, we cannot erase our sins by our own efforts. We are alienated from God and guilty in His holy eyes. The prophet Isaiah said, "But your iniquities have separated you from your God; your sins have hidden his face from you, so that he will not hear" (59:2). Only God can take away our sins; He made this possible by sending His only Son into the world to die for us. Because He was divine, Jesus Christ was without sin. But on the cross all our sins were placed on Him, and by His death He took upon Himself the judgment and Hell we deserve. He did for us what we could never do for ourselves, and now He freely offers us the gifts of forgiveness and eternal life if we will accept them. As Paul reminds us, "For the wages of sin is death, but the gift of God is eternal life in Christ Jesus our Lord" (Romans 6:23). Think of it: God now offers you the free gift of salvation—free because Jesus Christ has already paid the price for it.

When we come to Him and trust Him alone for our salvation, God forgives our sins, and we become reconciled to Him forever. He also comes to live within us by His Holy Spirit and adopts us into His family as His sons and daughters. And because we now belong to Him, we will be with Him in Heaven someday. In the meantime He is with us every moment of the day, to the very end of our earthly journey.

It is never too late to begin building your life on the foundation of Jesus Christ and His will for your life, "for no one can lay any foundation other than the one already laid, which is Jesus Christ" (1 Corinthians 3:11). Is He the foundation of your life?

## LIFE'S GREATEST DECISION

The first action a builder takes as he starts the actual construction of a new building is laying its foundation. He knows that if he skips that step, or if he fails to construct it properly, then that building—no matter how beautiful or impressive it may appear on the outside—is fatally flawed and simply will not last. Sooner or later it will weaken and collapse.

However, before he begins construction or even sets foot on the property, something else must first take place. That *something* is a decision—a personal commitment by the owner—to build the building. And this must be our first step. We all want a happy and secure life; we all want a solid and lasting foundation beneath us. But wishful thinking is not enough! We need to make a decision—a personal commitment to Jesus Christ and His will for our lives.

Have you committed your life to Jesus Christ? No matter how young or old you are, are you seeking to build your life on Him? The most important decision you will ever make is to give your life to Christ and become His follower. Don't wait until life's storms begin to batter you; then it may be too late. Open your heart and life to Him now. "Now is the time of God's favor, now is the day of salvation" (2 Corinthians 6:2).

If you have never invited Jesus Christ to come into your life, or if you are unsure of your salvation, I invite you to pause right now and ask Him to come into your life, to forgive you, and to save you—and He will. To help you make this commitment, I urge you to pray the following prayer right now (or something similar in your own words):

O God, I know I am a sinner. I am sorry for my sins, and I want to turn from them. I trust Jesus Christ as my Savior, I confess Him as my Lord, and I invite Him to come into my life today. From this moment on, I want to make Him the foundation of my life and to serve Him and follow Him in the fellowship of His church. In Christ's name I pray. Amen.

If you sincerely prayed this prayer, God heard you and forgave you—and you are now His child forever. You also have taken the first step in building your life on a solid foundation—one that will last not only throughout your life, but through all eternity. And from your commitment will come the moral and spiritual strength you need to face the challenges of the future.

## NEARING HOME WITH A SOLID FOUNDATION

When I think of the words J. W. Van DeVenter penned in 1896, the foundation of the Christian life comes to mind:

> All to Jesus, I surrender;
> All to Him I freely give;
> I will ever love and trust Him,
> In His presence daily live.

At the time of our personal surrender and acceptance of Jesus Christ as Lord and Savior, He commands us to walk in His footsteps. Receiving His power gives us courage to follow Him and abide in His presence.

The elderly should take heart in the biographies that fill the pages of Scripture and the foundations that have been laid by those who have lived before us. The Bible does not diminish old age but teaches its values and virtues. We would do well to emulate the wisdom of those who responsibly passed on the building blocks of God's truth.

Before Joshua died at age 110, he gathered those he had led and reminded them about the days of old: their disobedience and repentance and God's forgiveness and faithfulness. He made a proclamation that thousands of years later hangs in homes around the world: "But as for me and my house, we will serve the LORD" (Joshua 24:15 NKJV). Joshua did not shrink in old age, nor did he shirk his responsibility. He boldly reminded the people of the building blocks that will secure our foundation: "Fear the LORD, serve Him in sincerity and in truth" (Joshua 24:14 NKJV).

Instead of the elderly taking a backseat in the twilight years, we need to faithfully proclaim as Joshua did, "Incline your heart to the LORD God" (Joshua 24:23 NKJV). Perhaps those who are watching and listening would respond as those who listened to Joshua's wise counsel when they said, "The LORD our God we will serve, and His voice we will obey!" (Joshua 24:24 NKJV). The Bible says of Joshua that he had "known all the works of the LORD which He had done" (Joshua 24:31 NKJV). Our voices may be weak, but let our spirits be strong in reminding others that the root of God's love will grow deep in the hearts of all who will desire the Water of Life.

# 9 ROOTS STRENGTHEN IN TIME

So then, just as you received Christ Jesus as Lord,
continue to live in him, rooted and built up in him,
strengthened in the faith.

—COLOSSIANS 2:6–7

Anyone who stops learning is old, whether at twenty
or eighty.

—HENRY FORD

Our culture is not defined by the old or the new—but by
the latest. The high-tech world moves at accelerated speeds.
Society sharpens itself on the cutting edge that, at times, can be
deceitful. A cable news network recently carried a press conference

on the announcement of the new iPad. Before the presentation was finished, creators of the product told plans of its coming replacement. Keeping up with the latest and greatest is difficult.

This increasing pace of innovation is challenging, especially for those of us who are getting along in years. My generation saw life go from the Model T to the iEverything—the iPhone, iPod, iPad, iCard, iStore, iSource, and so on. We were taught to take care of what we possessed, then pass it down to the young, hoping that they would cherish what had meaning. Youth, however, are accustomed to discarding one possession for another that might look the same but possess something unseen: more memory. In a world already drowning in the information flood, tech companies are constantly increasing memory capacity, and users are thrilled at forgetting the old to make room for the new. Meanwhile the older generation is hanging on for dear life to the memories we have accumulated during our lifetimes, fearful we might forget the anchors that stabilized, the lighthouse that directed, and the Word of God that calmed the treacherous waters.

A popular technology accessory company posted on its website, "We are surrounded by so much technology that we begin to forget our roots."[1] That's quite an admission. It's true. People can become so encumbered with being "connected" to information that they "disconnect" from others. Technology can weaken relationships and push the reality of life out of the way. Generally, the older someone is, the more intensely this disconnect is felt, especially from the young. I encourage those who are grandparents to never give up on seeking creative ways to engage your grandchildren. Remember, the oldest generation may struggle with short-term memory loss, but its attention span is probably still greater than that of younger generations. Let's remember to teach them by example that roots are important. It is our responsibility to build them up: "Encourage one another and build one another up" (1 Thessalonians 5:11 ESV).

Generations that are younger in years cope with boredom more than my generation did. Something new to us remained new and valued for a long time. But eventually, newness wears off. Within days after a baby is born, the cherished whimper to new parents becomes the nagging whine. A toddler's first steps, once applauded for getting to where they want to go, are soon scolded when they lead to someplace unsafe. King Solomon in his wisdom predicted this quick dissatisfaction with the latest and greatest when he wrote,

> The eye is not satisfied with seeing,
> Nor the ear filled with hearing. . . .
> There is nothing new under the sun.
> Is there anything of which it may be said,
> "See, this is new"?
> It has already been in ancient times before us. (Ecclesiastes
> 1:8–10 NKJV)

While we all benefit in some ways from modern technology, I do wonder what state our world would be in if we suddenly lost the electrical power necessary to keep our communications functioning. Would the younger generations know how to grow crops to feed a family? Would they know how to drop anchor and wait for the catch? Would they know how to survive by the sweat of the brow? New is good. Old is necessary.

The Bible has a lot to say about the old and the new. "I write no new commandment to you, but an old commandment which you have had from the beginning. The old commandment is the word which you heard from the beginning" (1 John 2:7 NKJV). In this text John is reminding his readers that the proof of knowing God is following the commandments that He gave long ago, that He gave "from the beginning." The love of God is then perfected in the one who obeys (1 John 2:5 NKJV). Anything "from the beginning" is old, including God's love, present before the beginning of time. When man did not fathom the inexpressible love of God the Creator, He sent love down to earth in the form of His Son, the Lord Jesus Christ. Our redemption is rooted in Jesus' sacrifice of Himself, keeping us firmly planted.

## GROWING FROM SEED TO SEEDLING

Growing anything takes time. It takes planning. It takes commitment. There is something gratifying in tilling soil, planting seed, watering roots, and watching the sun raise a plant from the soil. It is satisfying to break ground, erect an infrastructure, and nail down a roof. A stopwatch cannot count down the months it takes to see the results. Patience has become a lost virtue. One hundred years ago the hourglass marked time. Today, if the iconic hourglass remains on the computer screen longer than a few seconds, it causes undue stress for the student or executive who has no time for contemplation.

I have always admired those who work with their hands. When a friend of mine retired years ago, he and his wife began researching where they might retire. A prerequisite was finding a place where he could have a woodworking shop. Still today he makes beautiful bowls and candlesticks from old wood he finds while hiking in nearby forests.

"What is your favorite wood to work with?" I asked him one day.

"I suppose it would be from the trees that grow along the ridgetops of the Appalachian Mountains," he answered.

"Why?"

"Because of the harsh climate, those trees grow very slowly," he replied. "As a result the wood is tough and close-grained, which makes it hard to carve; but anything made from it will be durable and very beautiful."

That surprised me because I had often hiked past similar trees that were stunted and twisted into grotesque shapes by the fierce, cold winds that frequently buffet the peaks of Mount Mitchell, the highest point in the United States east of the Mississippi River, a dozen or so miles from my home. But when he showed me a box he had carved from this type of wood, I understood that what was once ugly and battered could be made into something exquisite by a masterful hand. I asked him to show me a piece of the rough wood.

"I haven't any right now. You see, I won't cut such trees down. I wait until they fall, and then I retrieve them and turn the wood into something beautiful."

Like those trees along our windswept mountain ridges, we often find ourselves buffeted by storms—the storms of life. Like those trees, we need deep roots that will supply us with the spiritual nutrients needed to grow strong in our faith and to keep us anchored when we are tossed about by life's trials.

Our country and our world have experienced one catastrophic storm after another the past few years. I revised and updated my book *Storm Warning*[2] in 2010 to heighten awareness of what the Bible has to say about storms in our world, storms in our lives, and the storms to come. As we get older, we encounter storms that we never thought we'd face. But with God's help and by His grace, we can be strong when the winds begin to blow.

It is no accident that the Bible compares us to trees, urging us to be sure our spiritual roots are deep and strong. The psalmist wrote that the godly person "is like a tree planted by streams of water, which yields its fruit in season" (Psalm 1:3). But a tree wasn't always a tree. It began as a small seed, which in time sprouted and became a seedling. If conditions were right, that fragile seedling grew into a sapling and finally into a mature tree.

The same is true of spiritual life. It begins with a seed—the seed of God's Word planted in the soil of our souls that eventually sprouts and becomes a new seedling. But—like a tree—that spiritual seedling isn't meant to remain a seedling forever! It is meant to grow and become strong and mature, bearing fruit that is pleasing to God. The Bible illustrates this truth in another way. When we come to Christ, the Bible says, we are like newborn babies—bursting with new life, but helpless and weak and vulnerable to every kind of danger. But a baby isn't meant to remain that way forever. Infants are meant to grow and eventually become adults—no longer helpless and weak and vulnerable, but able to take care of themselves and have full and productive lives.

The same is true for us spiritually. When we come to Christ, we are born again—that is, God our Heavenly Father works in our hearts by His Holy Spirit to give us new life as His children (John 3:1–17). But we aren't meant to remain spiritual infants, weak and vulnerable to every temptation or doubt or falsehood or fear. God's will is for us to grow strong in our faith and become spiritually mature, grounded in the truth of His Word and firmly committed to doing His will. The Bible says, "Like newborn babies, crave pure spiritual milk, so that by it you may grow up in your salvation" (1 Peter 2:2).

Giving your life to Christ is an essential first step—but it is only the first step. God's will is for you to become spiritually mature, growing stronger in your relationship to Christ and your service for Him. But this takes both time and effort. Conversion is the work of an instant; spiritual maturity is the work of a lifetime. It is a journey with many steps, and it should be everyone's main goal in life. Is it yours?

## BECOMING MORE LIKE HIM

What is spiritual maturity? To put it another way, what does God want to do in our lives? What does He want to do in your life?

The Bible's answer can be put in one sentence: God's will is for us to become more and more like the Lord Jesus Christ. He wants to change us from within, taking away everything that dishonors Him and replacing it with Christ's love and purity. From all eternity God's plan was that we would be "conformed to the likeness of his Son, that he might be the firstborn among many brothers"

(Romans 8:29). This is spiritual maturity: to become more and more like Christ in our "love, joy, peace, patience, kindness, goodness, faithfulness, gentleness and self-control" (Galatians 5:22–23).

Will we ever reach this goal? No, not completely in this life—but someday we will enter God's presence forever, and then we will be totally free from sin's grip. Then "we shall be like him, for we shall see him as he is" (1 John 3:2).

So what about the present? Does this mean it is hopeless to strive for spiritual maturity? No! God wants to begin changing us from within and making us more like Christ right now. In Heaven that process will be complete; sin's power over us will be destroyed, and we will inherit that Heavenly home Christ has prepared for us. Do you want to know what God's will is for you? It is simply this: to become more like Christ. Do others see Christ in you?

## DEVELOPING A ROOT SYSTEM

How can we develop a faith that will be strong enough to see us through the whole of our lives, including the uncertainties and challenges of old age?

The key is this: God wants us to be spiritually strong and has provided us with every resource we need. In ourselves we are weak, so if we try to meet life's struggles and temptations on our own, we fail. We need God's strength to face life's challenges—and He wants to give it to us. He will strengthen us in faith as we make use of the resources He has given us; He will develop a root system within us that grabs hold of surety. As Peter reminded us, "His divine power has given us everything we need for life and godliness through our knowledge of him who called us by his own glory and goodness" (2 Peter 1:3).

Tragically, many Christians never discover this. They have committed their lives to Christ . . . they may be active in their churches . . . they pray and read their Bibles on occasion—but they remain spiritually immature and weak in the face of life's temptations and setbacks. The Bible warns us about the danger of remaining spiritual infants "tossed back and forth by the waves, and blown here and there by every wind of teaching and by the cunning and craftiness of men in their deceitful scheming" (Ephesians 4:14).

We may be old in years, but if our faith is immature, we will enter those latter years fearful and unprepared. But it doesn't need to be this way. Just as a baby needs food and exercise in order to grow, so we need the spiritual food and exercise God has provided for us. Without them our faith is weak, but with them spiritual strength increases, and we are better prepared for whatever life has in store for us.

How do we grow strong in our faith? What spiritual resources has God given us to make this happen? In the next few pages I would like to examine five of these gifts.

## The Gift of God's Word

Some years ago Ruth was visiting one of our daughters, and she decided to build a rudimentary zip line for the grandchildren. Always adventurous, she secured a sturdy wire at an angle between two trees. To test it she climbed the tree at the taller end, grabbed the handle (made from a piece of pipe), and started down the inclined wire.

But the wire broke, hurtling her to the ground some fifteen feet below. She broke several bones, crushed a vertebra, and suffered a severe brain concussion that left her in a coma for a week. As she slowly recovered, she realized that large blocks of her memory were missing—including all the Bible verses she had memorized since childhood. "That was the worst part," she said later. "The Bible meant so much to me and had guided me all my life, and now I couldn't even remember a single verse. It was devastating." I understood her heartache; I would have felt the same way in her place. Thankfully, over time her memory largely returned, including—little by little—the Bible verses she had learned over the years.

Why was the Bible so important to her? And why should it be important to us? The reason is simple: the Bible is God's Word, given by God to teach us His truth and guide us through life. The Bible says,

> I am the LORD your God,
>> who teaches you what is best for you,
>> who directs you in the way you should go. (Isaiah 48:17)

The Bible is not an option; it is a necessity if we are going to be rooted in Him.

How does the Bible help us develop spiritually? First, it points us to the truth—about God, about ourselves, about the world around us, about the future, and most of all about Jesus Christ and His love for us. Only Jesus—the incarnate Son of God—could say, "I am the way and the truth and the life. No one comes to the Father except through me. . . . Anyone who has seen me has seen the Father" (John 14:6, 9). The Christian faith isn't just a matter of personal opinion or unfounded optimism. It is rooted in the unchanging truth of God, revealed to us in the pages of His written Word. The Bible is the constant rain that waters our root system of faith. It is the inspiration from which we drink daily.

The Bible then nourishes our growing roots with principles to live by. Every day we face decisions—some insignificant but others of great importance (although we may not realize it at the time). How can we be sure we make the right decisions? By applying biblical principles. The psalmist reminds us, "How can a young man keep his way pure? By living according to your word" (Psalm 119:9). The world has its own values and goals: self-gratification, success, pleasure, security, pride, and so forth. But these are false, and they will never give us the lasting security and peace we seek.

In His guidebook God gives us a different set of values and goals—ones that put Christ at the center of our lives instead of self. The Bible tells us to flee from sin and self-indulgence, and seek instead to base our lives on "righteousness, godliness, faith, love, endurance and gentleness" (1 Timothy 6:11). The Bible also gives us practical wisdom for daily living. It is our instructor, showing us how to live. For many years I made it a practice to read a chapter a day from the book of Proverbs, thus covering the entire book every month. Proverbs is filled with practical wisdom on a wide variety of topics: relationships, possessions, family, speech, work, habits, and so much more. "The ways of the LORD are right; the righteous walk in them" (Hosea 14:9). The Bible is our authority in everything.

From one end to the other, God's Word is filled with promises—promises concerning His unchanging love, His presence, His help, His peace in times of turmoil. Most of all, the Bible promises us that someday we will go to be with God in Heaven forever because of what Jesus Christ has done for us. Learn God's promises, trust them, and live by them every day, for God "has given us his very great and precious promises, so that through them you may participate in the divine nature and escape the corruption in the world caused by evil desires" (2 Peter 1:4).

Are you seeking to base your life on the principles and values God has given us in the Bible? Don't be intimidated by it or think it is impossible to understand. Even if you read only a few verses a day, God can still use it to reshape your life. Take advantage of opportunities to learn the Bible from others—your pastor, respected teachers on Christian radio, Bible studies and conferences, and Christian books; but never let these things replace your personal reading of Scripture.

## The Gift of the Holy Spirit

When we come to Jesus Christ and put our faith and trust in Him, God Himself comes to live within us. We may not feel any different; we may be unaware of His presence; we may even doubt if anything has really happened to us. But it has. God now lives within us! He does this through His Holy Spirit.

Just as Jesus is fully God, so, too, the Holy Spirit is fully God. Although we can't see Him, He is that part of God who is working and active in our world. He isn't an impersonal force (like gravity); He is a person, just as God the Father and Christ the

Son are persons—that is, they are personal in their natures. (This, incidentally, is why we shouldn't refer to the Holy Spirit as "it" but as "He.")

Why does God the Holy Spirit come to live within us when we give our lives to Christ? One reason is to assure us of our salvation. How do we know Christ has forgiven all our sins and given us the gift of eternal life? We know it because the Bible says so—and the Holy Spirit confirms in our hearts that this is true. The Bible says, "The Spirit himself testifies with our spirit that we are God's children" (Romans 8:16).

God has also given us the Holy Spirit to help us discover God's will. Certainly the Bible gives us principles to live by, helping us avoid wrong and do what is right. But often we face choices that seem equally good, and we need to know which is right. Should we change jobs? Sell our house? Marry this person? Retire? The list is almost endless because life is filled with decisions. God wants to guide us as we make those decisions because He loves us and wants us to have what is best for us. God's promise is sure: "Whether you turn to the right or to the left, your ears will hear a voice behind you, saying, 'This is the way; walk in it'" (Isaiah 30:21). The Holy Spirit illuminates our minds and makes us yearn for God. He takes spiritual truth and makes it understandable to us.

The Holy Spirit also has been given to us to encourage and strengthen us in times of trouble. "The Spirit helps us in our weakness" (Romans 8:26), and this includes more than just helping us as we pray. When hard times come, He may bring to mind passages of Scripture that assure us of God's love and protection. When temptations assail us, the Spirit strengthens us and gives us courage to fight our adversary, the devil. Paul prayed that God "out of his glorious riches . . . may strengthen you with power through his Spirit in your inner being" (Ephesians 3:16).

Finally, the Holy Spirit has come to change us from within. God wants to change our lives, to make us more like Christ. It is never a question of how much we have of the Spirit but of how much He has of us. The Bible says, "Do not conform any longer to the pattern of this world, but be transformed by the renewing of your mind" (Romans 12:2). Is this happening in your life?

Don't try to fight the battle of the Christian life in your own strength. Instead turn to God in submission and faith, and trust His Holy Spirit to help you.

## The Gift of Prayer

Some people look on prayer as a burden or obligation, but in reality prayer is one of our greatest privileges as God's children. Think of it: the God of the universe wants us to bring every concern to Him in prayer! I have never met anyone who spent time in daily prayer, studied God's Word regularly, and was strong in faith who was ever discouraged for very long. The Bible says, "Do not be anxious about anything, but in everything, by prayer and petition, with thanksgiving, present your requests to God. And the peace of God, which transcends all understanding, will guard your hearts and your minds in Christ Jesus" (Philippians 4:6–7).

Does God always answer our prayers the way we wish He would? No, not necessarily—nor has He promised to do so. He sees the whole picture, but we don't; He knows what is best for us, but we often don't. Sometimes, therefore, He says no, or "Not now."

But God has promised to hear us when we pray and to answer our prayers in His time and in His way: "This is the confidence we have in approaching God: that if we ask anything according to his will, he hears us" (1 John 5:14).

Remember, however, that prayer isn't just asking for things we want. Prayer is for every moment of our lives, not just for times of suffering or joy. Prayer is really a place, a place where you meet God in genuine conversation. True prayer includes thanking and praising Him for who He is and all He does. The Bible tells us in 1 Thessalonians 5:17 to "pray continually"—and not just when we are facing a crisis or want God to do something for us. No matter how dark and hopeless a situation may seem, never stop praying. Prayer should be an attitude of life. We cannot afford to be too busy to pray.

I often receive letters from invalids and older people who say, "All I can do is pray." I've often answered back, "God bless you for doing the most important thing." I can remember the comfort I felt in my early years of ministry just knowing that my mother was home praying for me. It strengthened me, and God used that information to help me stay focused and committed to the task He had given me. We need armies of pray-ers.

## The Gift of Fellowship

We are not meant to be isolated from and independent of each other, either as human beings or as Christians. We need other people in our lives, and they need us. This is especially true as we seek to grow in faith. The Bible says, "Let us not give up meeting together, as some are in the habit of doing, but let us encourage one another" (Hebrews 10:25). A solitary Christian is inevitably a weak Christian because he or she is failing to draw strength from what God is doing in the lives of fellow brothers and sisters in Christ.

If you aren't presently part of a church fellowship, ask God to guide you to a church where you can grow in your faith through biblical preaching and teaching and worship. The church is a storehouse of spiritual food. This is where our souls are fed, nourished, and developed into maturity. It is there we can "encourage one another and build each other up" (1 Thessalonians 5:11).

## The Gift of Service

Just as our bodies need exercise to be strong physically, our faith needs exercise if we are to be strong spiritually.

It has often been noted that several rivers flow into the Dead Sea, but no river flows from it. That's why its water has become so saturated with minerals over the centuries that nothing is able to live in it. Without any outlet it indeed has become a "dead" sea. The same is true with us. If we keep faith to ourselves, if we never allow it to flow through us to enrich others, and if it has no outlet, then we will find ourselves like the Dead Sea—lifeless and spiritually dead.

God wants to use you right where you are. Every day you probably come into contact with people who will never enter a church or talk with a pastor or open a Bible. You may be the bridge God uses to bring them to His Son, the Lord Jesus Christ. Anyone can be a servant, no matter how inadequate he or she may feel. Moses himself protested that he could not speak for God because he was ineloquent, maybe suffering from a speech impediment

(Exodus 4:10). A wonderful friend Dr. Irmhild Bärend, who serves as our editor for *Decision* magazine in Germany, became paralyzed some years ago. In spite of her hardships, she has a countenance that radiates her love for Christ. She is grateful for every trip to see her doctors, therapists, or caregivers because, as she says to our mutual friends, "If I were not in this wheelchair, I would not have the privilege to tell them about Jesus."

## STANDING STRONG

A young purple-leaf plum tree seemed the perfect choice: its color matched the other landscaping, and a neighbor in my community thought it would grow to shade the hot eastern corner of her home. She was wrong. Five years after planting it, the tree was stunted. It was frequently sick—attacked by insects and struck with blights—and worse, it would lean until its branches touched the ground in any strong wind. No matter how she staked it, it would not stand tall against the elements. She complained about this to a friend, so he examined the tree and identified the problem—it had never taken root. Planted close to a downspout, the tree never needed to stretch its roots beyond its infant root ball to find water. It eventually would die.

Contrast this tree with the maple sapling planted on the edge of her property the same spring. A bare-root plant, the sapling was forced to reach up for sun and out for water. Five years later, it was taller than the stunted plum tree and healthy. The Christian life should look like the life cycle of that maple sapling. After our roots of faith are planted in the fertile ground of truth, we should grow strong as we understand God's Word, draw close to the Holy Spirit, talk to God daily in prayer, and fellowship with our brothers and sisters in Christ. As we drink from the springs of life, our roots will grow deeper when we are serving Christ. Only with a deep root system can we endure the storms of life and prepare the next generations to follow in our footsteps.

## NEARING HOME WITH A MATURE FAITH

Strengthening our spiritual roots begins with God's Word. Many have said that when they were young, they were too busy to read the Bible and memorize Scripture. Before they realized it, they had grown old and could not commit Bible verses to memory because their memories failed them. That may be true for some, but not for everyone. Many of us remember what we want to remember.

A wonderful friend of ours, Robert Morgan, wrote a little book recently about Bible memorization and states, "Our minds are vaults especially designed to stockpile the seeds of God's Word." In his book, he tells the story of an eighty-nine-year-old woman in his church who said, "Oh, Pastor Morgan, I'm so glad you are having us memorize [Bible] verses. I've already gotten started on them. It's going to help me keep my mind fresh and young!"[3] It made me smile to realize that she would keep her mind fresh and young . . . she had not allowed it to get old. There is no better deposit to make in the human mind and heart than to fill them with the treasures found in the Word of God.

We see the results of committing God's Word to memory in

the lives of Simeon and Anna, who witnessed the presentation of the Child Jesus at the Temple (Luke 2:27). Because they knew the ancient Old Testament prophecies and believed by faith that a Savior would be born in Israel, the Holy Spirit revealed the Christ Child to them in their old age. Simeon, an old man who did not want to die before knowing the Savior had come into the world, took Jesus in his arms and blessed Him, saying, "Lord, now You are letting Your servant depart in peace, according to Your word; for my eyes have seen Your salvation which You have prepared before the face of all peoples" (Luke 2:29–31 NKJV). Anna, "a widow of about eighty-four years . . . served God with fastings and prayers night and day . . . and spoke of Him to all those who looked for redemption" (Luke 2:37–38 NKJV). In the story of Simeon and Anna, we see these gifts of God's Word, the Holy Spirit, prayer, fellowship, and service all working together to bring about remarkable blessings, and it all started with having their hearts and minds saturated with God's Word.

My heart is always moved when I read in Scripture of the faith of the elderly. Are the truths of God nourishing your root system? We may retire from our careers, but we must never retire from being filled with the abundant gifts from God that bring hope and satisfaction.

# 10 THEN AND NOW

Now we know that if the earthly tent we live in is destroyed, we have a building from God, an eternal house in heaven, not built by human hands.

—2 Corinthians 5:1

The last chapter in life can be the best.

—Vance Havner

We never know at what stage, or age, we are living the last chapter of life. Some do not survive birth. Others are taken in their youth. Many are snatched from this earth in the prime of life.

I never thought I would outlive my wife of sixty-three years, my dear Ruth, who passed from this life of uncertainty to the place she was assured to see—the beautiful shores of Heaven and the blessed face of the Master she lived for and served. One of my saddest moments was when Ruth preceded me in death. I watched her suffer with dignity, with feisty humor, and with a gentle spirit ready to meet our Lord. She taught me so much about the last chapter of life. Knowing where she is, the One she is with, and the fact that I will be there with her soon are of monumental comfort to me.

When I preached my last stadium crusade in New York's Flushing Meadows in 2005, I certainly did not dream that I would be living without Ruth two short years later. I truly believed that my declining health would not sustain many more years of life. In spite of the fact that we were apart for long periods of time over the span of six decades because of my intensive preaching schedule, I never contemplated living without Ruth. Throughout our marriage the telephone was about the only thing that came between us, and I was always grateful to hear her voice. Now to be without her in our home at Little Piney Cove would be more than I could bear if it were not for the fact that she left so much of herself behind. She oversaw the construction of our log house more than fifty years ago, and to this day, touches of Ruth are in every room. Missing her the past four years has taught me things I would have never learned, many from Ruth even in her absence. And because she wrote from the depths of her soul with strokes of her winsome personality, she still makes me smile.

> This old house is empty now,
> with mostly only me,
> the trees are crowding up the hill
> as if for company.[1]

This reflected her thoughts after all the children were gone, what is now called *empty-nest syndrome*. Ruth simply called it what it was: *then and now.* I watched how she transitioned from one stage of life to another with grace.

God designs transitions and provides the grace to embrace what follows. When Jesus prepared to leave His earthly dwelling to return to Glory, He told His beloved disciples, "I am going away. . . . If you loved Me, you would rejoice because I said, 'I am going to the Father'" (John 14:28 NKJV). "I am the way, the truth, and the life. No one comes to the Father except through Me" (John 14:6 NKJV). And Jesus instructed them, giving them work to do: "Feed my sheep" (John 21:17), "Follow me" (John 21:19), and "Be my witnesses" (Acts 1:8). He didn't just abandon His disciples; Jesus guided them toward the work they needed to do for the Kingdom so the church would not suffer and the disciples themselves would remain focused on Jesus' work even after He returned to the Father. How wonderful that the Lord did not leave the world void of His presence but sent His Holy Spirit to be our constant companion.

While I will never grow accustomed to life without Ruth, she would be the first to scold me if I didn't look for God's plan for the *here and now.* This was her realm. It would be easy to sit and reminisce about all that was accomplished during the years of public ministry. I am grateful, for I know that "such mighty works are performed by His hands!" (Mark 6:2 NKJV). But I also know that God has a purpose in everything, and He will guide us into whatever He has for us if our hearts, minds, and eyes are watching and waiting attentively.

In all my years traveling from coast to coast, from country to country, I seldom had time to watch television. That was *then.*

*Now* my eyesight is failing, and watching television is difficult. Getting to church is not easy either. So I am thankful for those who faithfully preach the Word of God on television, where I can at least hear a good sermon from Scripture. I have been personally blessed by those the Lord is using to minister to the elderly who are no longer able to attend church.

I began listening to a telecast from Spartanburg, South Carolina. Dr. Don Wilton, senior pastor of First Baptist Church, began ministering to my heart through his messages, and I found myself looking forward to the next Sunday's program. Some months later, I called to thank him for his ministry and invited him to my home. We enjoyed wonderful fellowship together. Since that time, he has graciously driven ninety miles from Spartanburg for a visit every week. We have lunch together and discuss everything from family to world events. But the most meaningful part of our visits is when we look into the Scriptures together and spend time in prayer. Often he shares a sermon outline he is working on and with enthusiasm asks for my thoughts. There have been times I have asked for his assistance with thoughts on various passages as I prepare statements and brief talks. It is a great privilege for me to have fellowship with a great teacher of Scripture and to feel a unity of purpose and desire to see others come to Christ. This is the work God has for all of His people—*now*.

## DON'T LIVE WITHOUT HOPE

We were not meant for this world alone. We were meant for Heaven, our final home. Heaven is our destiny, and Heaven is our joyous hope. In reality not everyone agrees with this. "You are free to have your own opinion," a young man wrote me recently, "but as far as I'm concerned once you are dead, that's it. When we die we're no different from an animal lying by the side of the road. The only life we'll ever experience is the one we're living right now. Life after death is just a myth."

My reply came from the bottom of my heart. "Your letter deeply saddened me," I wrote, "because it means you are living without hope—hope for this life, and hope for the life to come. Have you honestly faced how empty and meaningless this will make your life?" I then urged him to turn to Jesus Christ and put his life into His hands, for He alone can give us hope for the future. What would our lives be like without any hope of life beyond the grave?

Death is a reality, but death was not part of God's original plan. When God created Adam and Eve, He gave them physical bodies, just like every other creature on earth. But one thing made them different: God not only gave them a body, but He also implanted within them a soul, a spirit, made in His image. He did this so they could know Him and become His friends, and because of this they were meant to live forever. God cannot die, and as the bearers of His image, they were not meant to die either.

But something terrible intervened, and that *something* was sin. Sin, like a lethal spiritual cancer, has infected the entire human race, and someday you and I will die. It may be soon, it may be far away, but someday your life will come to an end. At one specific point in time, the body you have inhabited your entire life will cease functioning and begin to disintegrate, and the words spoken to Adam will become true of you also: "For dust you are and to dust you will return" (Genesis 3:19). No wonder the Bible calls death "the last enemy" (1 Corinthians 15:26).

But is death really the end? Was the young man right when he said life after death is just a myth? No—absolutely not. The Bible tells us that although our bodies will die, our souls or spirits will live on—either in Heaven with God or in that place of endless loneliness and despair the Bible calls Hell, totally separated from God and His blessings forever. Jesus warned, "Do not be afraid of those who kill the body but cannot kill the soul. Rather, be afraid of the One who can destroy both soul and body in hell" (Matthew 10:28).

## THIS PRESENT LIFE IS NOT THE END

But how do we know this life isn't the end? How do we know Heaven isn't just wishful thinking on our part? God has revealed Heaven's reality to us in various ways. For example, within each of us is an inner sense or feeling that death is not the end, that there must be something beyond the grave. Even if we deny it or ignore it, this inner yearning is still there—and it is universal. Where did it come from? The Bible says God placed it within us: He "set eternity in the hearts of men" (Ecclesiastes 3:11). Some point to the reports of people who claim to have been given a glimpse of Heaven, often as they were dying. While such accounts must be treated with caution, I have no doubt that it does happen on occasion; my own maternal grandmother had a vision of Jesus welcoming her into Heaven as she lay dying.

The final proof of Heaven's reality, however, comes from Jesus

Christ. Repeatedly He told His disciples not only that Heaven exists, but that someday they would go there. To Lazarus's sisters He declared, "I am the resurrection and the life. He who believes in me will live, even though he dies; and whoever lives and believes in me will never die" (John 11:25–26). He promised His disciples, "In my Father's house are many rooms; if it were not so, I would have told you. I am going there to prepare a place for you . . . that you also may be where I am" (John 14:2–3). The best-known verse in all the Bible underlines this truth: "For God so loved the world that he gave his one and only Son, that whoever believes in him shall not perish but have eternal life" (John 3:16).

How can we know—beyond a shadow of doubt—that there is life after death? The only way would be for someone to die—and then come back to life and tell us what lies beyond the grave. And that's exactly what happened when Jesus Christ rose again from the dead. It was the most unique and startling event in all history, and because of it we know that death is not the end, and we can be assured of eternal life. The Bible says, "For the wages of sin is death, but the gift of God is eternal life in Christ Jesus our Lord" (Romans 6:23).

More than that, however, Jesus' death and resurrection tell us that sin and death have been defeated forever. We do not need to fear the grave because by His death and resurrection, Jesus Christ has opened Heaven's door for us. The Bible says, "Praise be to the God and Father of our Lord Jesus Christ! In his great mercy he has given us new birth into a living hope through the resurrection of Jesus Christ from the dead, and into an inheritance that can never perish, spoil or fade—kept in heaven for you" (1 Peter 1:3–4). These words, penned by the apostle Peter near the end of his life, are God's promise to you and to all who put their faith and trust in Jesus Christ as their Lord and Savior. Yes, Heaven is real!

## WHAT IS HEAVEN LIKE?

I don't believe I have ever known a person (or at least a Christian) who did not want to know what Heaven is like—including me! This is not mere curiosity, however, like wondering about some place we have never visited. Instead we know that Heaven is our final home—the place where we will be spending all eternity. Why wouldn't we want to know what Heaven will be like?

Admittedly the Bible doesn't answer all our questions about Heaven. One reason, I've realized, is that Heaven is so much greater than anything our limited minds can ever imagine. Even if God answered all our questions about Heaven, we wouldn't be able to understand them! The Bible says,

> No eye has seen,
>   no ear has heard,
> no mind has conceived
>   what God has prepared for those who love him.
>   (1 Corinthians 2:9)

Only in Heaven will we be able to grasp completely its endless glory and wonder and joy. Then, the Bible says, we "will share in the glory to be revealed" (1 Peter 5:1).

But even if the Bible doesn't tell us everything we want to

know about Heaven, it does tell us everything we *need* to know. And everything—without exception—that it tells us about Heaven should make us want to go there! (On the other hand, everything— without exception—that the Bible tells us about Hell should make us *not* want to go there.) What, then, is Heaven like? The Bible tells us at least five important truths about Heaven.

## Heaven Is Glorious

We sometimes speak of a beautiful sunset or a warm spring day as "glorious," but even earth's most awe-inspiring nature is but a shadow of the glory of Heaven. When the apostle John was given a glimpse of Heaven's grandeur, he barely could find words to describe it, comparing it to the most wondrous objects on earth—only far greater: "It shone with the glory of God, and its brilliance was like that of a very precious jewel, like a jasper, clear as crystal. . . . The great street of the city was of pure gold, like transparent glass. . . . The city does not need the sun or the moon to shine on it, for the glory of God gives it light, and the Lamb [Christ] is its lamp" (Revelation 21:11, 21, 23).

Why is Heaven glorious? It isn't simply because of its incredible beauty, overwhelming as that will be. Heaven is glorious for one supreme reason: Heaven is the dwelling place of God. "And I heard a loud voice from the throne saying, 'Now the dwelling of God is with men, and he will live with them. They will be his people, and God himself will be with them and be their God.' . . . They will see his face, and his name will be on their foreheads" (Revelation 21:3; 22:4). Think of it: if you know Jesus Christ, someday you will be safely in God's presence forever! I can barely imagine what that will be like—but it will be glorious beyond description.

## Heaven Is Perfect

Not only is Heaven glorious, but it is also perfect. This shouldn't surprise us: since God is perfect, so, too, is Heaven, His dwelling place.

Why is this important? Because it reminds us that in Heaven everything imperfect will be banished. As the Bible says, "When perfection comes, the imperfect disappears" (1 Corinthians 13:10). Think of all the sins and evils that afflict us now: disease, death, loneliness, fear, sorrow, temptation, disappointment, disability, addiction, war, conflict, anger, jealousy, greed—the list is almost endless. But in Heaven all those will be banished! Every evil and sin will be destroyed; every doubt and fear will be removed; every disappointment and heartache will be healed. One of the Bible's greatest promises about Heaven declares, "He will wipe every tear from their eyes. There will be no more death or mourning or crying or pain, for the old order of things has passed away. . . . Nothing impure will ever enter it" (Revelation 21:4, 27).

The Bible tells us a final truth about Heaven's perfection: in Heaven we will be perfect—and someday so will all creation. Sin will no longer have any power over anything—for sin and Satan will be bound forever, and we will become like Christ. More than that, in God's time we will be given new bodies—perfect bodies like that of Jesus Christ after His resurrection, free from all the limitations and frailties of our present bodies. The Bible says, "Dear friends, now we are children of God, and what we will be has not yet been made known. But we know that when he appears, we shall be like him, for we shall see him as he is" (1 John 3:2).

This is true not only for us but also for all creation. Sin has affected everything—not just us but the whole created world.

Don't ever take sin lightly; its destructive power extends to every creature and every object in the universe. This is a staggering thought. But the story doesn't end there, for the Bible promises that someday the whole creation will come to an end, and it "will be liberated from its bondage to decay and brought into the glorious freedom of the children of God" (Romans 8:21). I can't help but wonder if one of the things God will have us do in Heaven is explore the limitless treasures that will be part of His new creation.

When will this happen? When will Christ appear again? Devout Bible scholars don't always agree on the details, but one fact is clear: someday Christ will come again to defeat all the forces of sin and evil and establish His supreme authority over the entire creation. Jesus Himself warned us against trying to set an exact timetable for His return: "No one knows about that day or hour, not even the angels in heaven, nor the Son, but only the Father" (Mark 13:32). In God's time this present world order will come to an end, and Christ will return to rule in power and glory and justice: "In keeping with his promise we are looking forward to a new heaven and a new earth, the home of righteousness" (2 Peter 3:13).

The fact of Christ's return should fill us with hope and joy and expectation. But Christ's return also should remind us of another truth: when Christ comes again, He will judge the world with perfect justice. On that day, the Bible says, those who have rebelled against God and rejected His offer of salvation in Christ "will go away to eternal punishment, but the righteous to eternal life" (Matthew 25:46). These are sobering words, and if you have never turned from your sins and opened your heart and life to Jesus Christ, I pray you will do so now, before it is too late. Don't gamble with your eternal soul!

## Heaven Is Joyous

Not only will Heaven be glorious and perfect, but it also will be joyous. How could it be anything less? Its glory, its perfection—these alone would be enough to bring us unimaginable joy. But Heaven will be joyous for other reasons also. King David declared, "You will fill me with joy in your presence, with eternal pleasures at your right hand" (Psalm 16:11).

Heaven will be a place of joyous reunion with all those who have gone to Heaven before us. I am often asked if we will recognize each other in Heaven—and my answer is always a resounding yes! Someday soon I know I will be reunited with all those in my family who are already in Heaven—and especially my dear wife, Ruth. King David confidently expressed this hope; after the death of his infant son, he declared, "Can I bring him back again? I will go to him" (2 Samuel 12:23). When Christ was transfigured and His Heavenly glory overwhelmed His earthly appearance, Moses and Elijah appeared from Heaven with Him in recognizable form (Matthew 17:1–3). The Bible tells us that in Heaven we won't be isolated spirits, separated from each other and floating aimlessly around the clouds (as cartoons sometimes suggest). Instead we will be united together in Heaven: "We who are still alive and are left will be caught up *together with them* in the clouds to meet the Lord in the air. And so *we* will be with the Lord forever" (1 Thessalonians 4:17, emphasis added).

Perhaps, however, you shrink back from this; you don't look forward to meeting someone who has hurt you or someone you have hurt. Don't worry about this, however. In Heaven they will be perfect—and so will you!

Heaven is joyous also because in Heaven all our questions will be answered. Life can be confusing, and every one of us has stood at the grave of a loved one or watched as a great evil seemed to be winning the day, asking, "Why, God? Why did You let this happen? Where are You? It doesn't make any sense." But someday all our doubts and questions will be resolved, and we will understand. Paul put it this way: "Now we see but a poor reflection as in a mirror; then we shall see face to face. Now I know in part; then I shall know fully, even as I am fully known" (1 Corinthians 13:12). As part of this we will be able to look back over our lives and rejoice in God's goodness and grace to us.

In addition, Heaven will be joyous because all our burdens will be lifted—never to return. One of the Bible's most comforting pictures of Heaven is that it will be a place of rest: "Blessed are the dead who die in the Lord from now on. . . . They will rest from their labor" (Revelation 14:13).

But the Bible tells us a final truth about Heaven's joy: our experience of Heaven will express itself in joyous worship. The writer of Hebrews expressed it this way: "You have come to Mount Zion, to the heavenly Jerusalem, the city of the living God. You have come to thousands upon thousands of angels in joyful assembly, to the church of the firstborn, whose names are written in heaven" (12:22–23). On this earth our worship is imperfect, incomplete, superficial—even dull or boring. It shouldn't be this way, of course; joyous worship should be part of every believer's daily experience as we focus on God's greatness, goodness, and glory. But in Heaven our worship will be perfect because we will see our Savior face-to-face. Although it is often overlooked, one of the central themes of the book of Revelation is Heaven's worship:

Then I heard every creature . . . singing:

"To him who sits on the throne and to the Lamb

be praise and honor and glory and power,

for ever and ever!" (Revelation 5:13)

## Heaven Is Active

"To be honest, I'm not even sure I want to go to Heaven," someone e-mailed me not long ago. "It sounds so boring, just sitting around on a cloud doing nothing." This is a serious misunderstanding of Heaven. In spite of the popular image, we won't be sitting on clouds and strumming harps. Instead the Bible says we will be busy. God will have work for us to do! "The throne of God and of the Lamb will be in the city, and his servants will serve him" (Revelation 22:3). The difference is that in this life we get tired and weary, but in Heaven we will never get tired because we will have unlimited energy to serve Christ.

What will we do? The Bible doesn't say exactly; if it did, we probably wouldn't understand it anyway! It does, however, tell us that God will grant us the privilege of participating in Christ's rule over all creation: "And they will reign [with Him] for ever and ever" (Revelation 22:5). We definitely won't be bored in Heaven!

My longtime associate and Crusade song leader Cliff Barrows jokingly told me once that in Heaven I will be unemployed while he will still have a job. The reason, he explained (with a twinkle in his eye), is that in Heaven there won't be any need for evangelists while the Heavenly choirs will still need someone to lead them. I assured him that I wasn't worried about it because I was confident

God would find something else for me to do. He might, I added, even change me into a choir director!

## Heaven Is Certain

Heaven is glorious, Heaven is perfect, Heaven is joyous, and Heaven is active; but can we know—really know—that it is also certain? Can we know *for certain* that we will go there when we die and that it will be our eternal home? The Bible says yes!

Only one thing will keep you out of Heaven, and that is your sin. God is absolutely pure and holy, and even one sin—just one—would be enough to banish you from His presence forever. But Jesus Christ came to take away your sins by His death on the cross and His resurrection from the dead. The Bible says, "The blood of Jesus, his Son, purifies us from all sin" (1 John 1:7).

As long as you trust in yourself—your goodness, your religious deeds, your inner hopes—for your salvation, you will never have any lasting assurance of your salvation. After all, how will you know if you have been good enough or religious enough? The answer is, you won't.

But salvation does not depend on our goodness; if it did, we could never be saved, for God's standard is nothing less than perfection. We can never be good enough because "whoever keeps the whole law and yet stumbles at just one point is guilty of breaking all of it" (James 2:10). Our salvation depends instead solely on Jesus Christ and what He has already done for us. Our faith and trust must be in Him, and not in ourselves.

Are you trusting Him alone for your salvation? If you aren't, or if you are unsure, I urge you to turn to Jesus Christ in repentance and faith today and by a simple prayer ask Him to come into your life as your Lord and Savior. The Bible says, "This is the testimony: God has given us eternal life, and this life is in his Son. He who has the Son has life; he who does not have the Son of God does not have life" (1 John 5:11–12). Don't let another day go by without Christ. Don't doubt God's promises about the certainty of Heaven, and don't doubt what Jesus Christ has already done to save you by His death and resurrection. When doubts assail you (and the devil will be sure they will), remember this: If you have put your faith and trust in Christ, you now belong to Him. You have been adopted into His family, and you are now His beloved son or daughter. Because of this, the Bible says, nothing "in all creation, will be able to separate us from the love of God that is in Christ Jesus our Lord" (Romans 8:39). You are now part of His family—forever!

## OUR FINAL HOME

It has been a great privilege for me to be an evangelist; my greatest joy has come from seeing people all over the world respond to the life-changing message of Jesus Christ. But on a personal level it has had its downside because I was away from home so much, sometimes for months at a time. But no matter how short or long the trip was, when I landed in Charlotte or Asheville, I knew I was nearing home. Home was a place of rest and peace; it also was a place of love and joy and security.

In a far greater way, Heaven is our home—our final home—our ultimate place of complete peace and security and joy forever. Here our homes are imperfect, even at best; sadly, for many people home may actually be a place of conflict and unhappiness. But this isn't true of Heaven. When we belong to Christ, we know that when we die we finally will be at peace—for we will be home. Paul's words to the Christians in Corinth apply to us as well: "As long as we are at home in the body we are away from the Lord . . . [but we] would prefer to be away from the body and at home with the Lord" (2 Corinthians 5:6, 8). Heaven is our hope, Heaven is our future, and Heaven is our home! I look forward to being home at last, and I pray you do also.

When life's burdens press upon you or its pressures seem almost more than you can bear, turn your heart toward your Heavenly home: "Yea, though I walk through the valley of the shadow of death, I will fear no evil: for thou art with me; thy rod and thy staff they comfort me. . . . Surely goodness and mercy shall follow me all the days of my life: and I will dwell in the house of the LORD for ever" (Psalm 23:4, 6 KJV). When your hopes and dreams fall apart or people disappoint you or turn against you, turn your heart toward your Heavenly home. And when the infirmities and struggles of old age threaten to overwhelm you, turn your heart toward your Heavenly home.

## NEARING HOME WITH ASSURANCE

This is certainly what Christ did—before He departed His earthly life, His mind was on home and bringing us with Him: "I came forth from the Father and have come into the world. Again, I leave the world and go to the Father" (John 16:28 NKJV). Jesus said to His disciples, "Where I am going you cannot follow Me now, but you shall follow Me afterward" (John 13:36 NKJV), and "I go to prepare a place for you. . . . I will come again and receive you to Myself; that where I am, there you may be also. And where I go you know, and the way you know" (John 14:2–4 NKJV).

My friend, do you know the way? Jesus told us, "I am the way, the truth, and the life. No one comes to the Father except through Me" (John 14:6 NKJV). No one ever grows too old to accept Christ's forgiveness and enter into His glorious presence. When we look back over our experiences along life's journey, we may have regrets about the choices we made, but remember, that was *then* . . . this is *now*. We may recall the times we have failed our families, but that was *then* . . . this is *now*. Some reading this book may say, "But I rejected Christ my whole life. It's too late for me." I say to you, my friend, that was *then* . . . this is *now*. The Bible's promises were true then, they are true now, and they will be true forever. "Behold, *now* is the accepted time; behold, *now* is the day of salvation" (2 Corinthians 6:2 NKJV, emphasis added).

For those who have received the most precious gift of Christ's redeeming blood . . . you have reason to look forward to the glories of Heaven, for you will be perfected, you will be joyful, you will once again be active, and right *now* you can be certain that you are *nearing home*.

# NOTES

## Chapter 3: The Impact of Hope

1. E. Stanley Jones, *Growing Spiritually* (Nashville: Abingdon, 1953), 313.
2. E. Stanley Jones, *The Divine Yes*, with Eunice Jones Matthews (Nashville: Abingdon, 1975).
3. Laura Hillenbrand, *Unbroken: A World War II Story of Survival, Resilience, and Redemption* (New York: Random House, 2010).

## Chapter 4: Consider the Golden Years

1. "Full Text of the Will of J. Pierpont Morgan: Will Executed Jan. 4, 1913—Codicil Executed Jan. 6, 1913—Died March 31, 1913," *New York Times*, April 20, 1913, http://query.nytimes.com/gst/abstract.html?res=FB0813F93A5D13738DDDA90A 94DC405B838DF1D3 (accessed June 26, 2011).

## Chapter 5: Fading Strength but Standing Strong

1. S. Jay Olshansky, Leonard Hayflick, and Bruce A. Carnes, "No Truth to the Fountain of Youth," *Scientific American*, June 2002, http://www.scientificamerican .com/article.cfm?id=no-truth-to-the-fountain-of-youth (accessed June 26, 2011).

## Chapter 7: Influencing the Impressionable

1. Carol Morello, "A new generation of caregivers takes control of kids," *Washington Post*, September 10, 2010, http://www.washingtonpost.com/wp-dyn/content /article/2010/09/09/AR2010090906576.html (accessed June 26, 2011).
2. Meredith Alexander, "Stanford conference invites young people to discuss aging," Stanford News Service, April 27, 2001, http://news.stanford.edu/pr/01/Aging502 .html (accessed June 26, 2011).
3. mshurn [pseud.], "Topic: can you differentiate the old generation from the new generation?" eNotes, accessed June 26, 2011, http://www.enotes.com/history/discuss /can-you-differentiate-old-generation-from-new-51515.

## Chapter 9: Roots Strengthen in Time

1. "Introducing Root Cases," Root Cases LLC, accessed June 23, 2011, www .rootcases.com.
2. Billy Graham, *Storm Warning: Whether Global Recession, Terrorist Threats, or Devastating Natural Disasters, These Ominous Shadows Must Bring Us Back to the Gospel*, rev. ed. (Nashville: Thomas Nelson, 2010).
3. Robert J. Morgan, *100 Bible Verses Everyone Should Know by Heart* (Nashville: Broadman & Holman, 2010), 42.

## Chapter 10: Then and Now

1. Ruth Bell Graham, *Clouds Are the Dust of His Feet* (Wheaton, IL: Crossway Books, 1992), 132.

# ABOUT THE AUTHOR

Billy Graham, the world-renowned author, preacher, and evangelist, has delivered the Gospel message to more people face-to-face than anyone in history and has ministered on every continent of the world in more than 185 countries. Millions have read his inspirational classics, including *Angels*, *Peace with God*, *Hope for the Troubled Heart*, *The Journey*, and *Storm Warning*.